- 001

DEAR AUDIENCE

DEAR AUDIENCE

A Guide to the Enjoyment of Theatre

by

Blanche Yurka

Drawings by Rafaello Busoni

PRENTICE HALL, INC.,
Englewood Cliffs, N.J.

To Marjorie Thayer,
in appreciation of
her guidance and help

Library of Congress Catalog Card Number: 59-14944

Printed in the United States of America
19702

Acknowledgements

THE AUTHOR wishes to express her grateful thanks for permission to reprint copyrighted material, to:

Sheldon Cheney for quotation from *The Art Theatre,* published by Alfred A. Knopf, Inc. (copyright 1925)

Harper and Brothers, Publishers: John van Druten, *Playwright at Work* (copyright 1952).

Little, Brown and Company, Publishers: Edith Hamilton, *Mythology* (copyright 1942).

Longmans, Green and Company, Inc., Publishers: Sheldon Cheney, *The Theatre* (copyright 1958).

Phaidon Press, Ltd., Publishers: Somerville Storey, *Rodin* (copyright 1951).

The New Yorker, for quotation from an article by Kenneth Tynan (January 31, 1959).

The New York Herald Tribune, for quotation from an article by Howard Teichmann (September 14, 1958).

The New York Times, for quotation from an article by Brooks Atkinson.

The author also wishes to specially thank the following individuals whose cooperation and help during the writing of *Dear Audience* is hereby gratefully acknowledged: Robert Bonnard, for his painstaking research and his unflagging enthusiasm; Elsa and Edwin Schallert, for their encouraging interest and their wise advice; George Freedley, Curator, Theatre Collection, The New York Public Library, for his valued criticism, and his staff at the Library for their unfailing courtesy and patience in answering many questions; Willard Swires and the headquarters staff of the American National Theatre and Academy, for making available the factual material concerning that organization; Elaine Haslett, a particularly perceptive member of "the audience," whose fresh outlook and zeal for the subject were immensely stimulating; Doctor Hugh Fellows, Professor of Speech, New York University, for his advice and assistance in preparing the informational section of the book; and, last but not least, all the wonderful artists of the theatre from whom I, as part of *their* audiences, have drawn incalculable inspiration through the years.

Contents

Dear Audience

BEFORE YOU START reading I want to tell you what this
book is not.

It is not a history of the theatre.

It is not a handbook on how to become an actor.

It is not an autobiography of an actress.

Instead, it is my attempt as an inveterate theatre-
goer to share with you some of the thrills, the excitement,
the deeply moving experiences I have lived through in a
lifetime of theatre on both sides of the curtain.

1

I want to do this because I know how theatre can enrich your life, just as it has mine; how it can expand your horizons, and open wide the door to a world of magic. For it is not only as a performer that the theatre has given me joy. Some of my most radiant hours have been spent in front of the curtain, hours illuminated by impressions that have the power to move me to this very day.

No one can discuss the entertainment world of today without talking about motion pictures and television. These are the mass communication media which bring to thousands of people their particular and sometimes their only form of theatre. But you will find, as I do, that all of these stem from the core, the fountainhead, of live theatre—from sources that had their beginnings in ancient lands long ago. For when the form of a play changes, it usually changes only in the *manner* in which it is presented. There are really surprisingly few fundamental differences in material.

Over the entrance of the Royal Danish Theatre in Copenhagen the following words are inscribed:

NOT ONLY FOR AMUSEMENT

The theatre I am going to talk about carries out this concept. It presents a range of subjects as wide as all humanity. But it can do this for you only if you are there to respond, for without you, the audience, there is no theatre. Even in the seeming separation of actor and audience in television shows or in the movies, you are represented by the director and his staff to whom, as a symbol of you, the performance must be submitted. And, of course, in many television shows you *are* a part of a live audience that listens and watches in studio or auditorium.

You, the audience, are of various ages and varying interests; yet you are that curious "one" whom we, the workers in the theatre, must face when the house lights have dimmed and the curtain has risen—a dark yet white-speckled mass of humanity. By some miracle of communication we must send out to your hearts, to your minds, and to your funny-bones, ideas and emotions with which you can become identified.

This is a miracle—one that is a never-ending surprise to me. And when the miracle fails to take place, when the circuit is not completed, when you do not become one with us, all our efforts have missed their goal. We have failed.

But the failure is not always our fault, nor even the fault of the playwright. You, the audience, have a share in the responsibility. Your receptiveness, your ability to respond to the images set before you, will be in direct proportion to how much you know of this fascinating world of make-believe and of the manner in which it functions. You will learn out of what worlds of the imagination this magic has evolved and grown into the theatre whose rich heritage we enjoy today.

This knowledge will equip you to become one of those who can *send the mind to range in space to far horizons of time and place.* If you do this you are taken beyond your own small needs, desires, frustrations, and fulfillments. You see that which was and that which is with keener insight and a more understanding heart.

In our contemporary theatre we have a breath-taking example of the power of a play to bring home to people a lesson that could not have been expressed so poignantly through any other kind of presentation. *The Diary of*

Anne Frank has been played throughout the world. That audiences in Germany have taken it to their hearts is perhaps the most surprising part of this amazing success story. Preachers have thundered from their pulpits countless diatribes against race hatred and persecution. Cries of "Guilty! Guilty!" have been heard from countless throats. None of these has moved to pity the entire civilized world as has the simply told story of a young girl confined in a garret, whose faith in the ultimate goodness of people stayed with her to the very door of a gas chamber.

Theatre offers you this touchstone of humanity by which you can become a more understanding human being, and because theatre is a world of magic, a kind of outpost of a world of emotion and imagination, I feel an intense desire to share with all of you who are uninitiated into its several smaller worlds some of the beauty with which it has flooded my own life.

The Family Tree

I N THE THEATRE histories of the future our age will appear as the period of the twenty-four-hour-a-day theatre, with something for everyone at any hour of the day. Shortly after dawn you may listen to a college professor discuss over the air the plays of ancient Greece. A little later, if you wish, you can tune in on a children's play, or watch a TV Western. A housewife, while busying herself with her tasks, can keep an ear or an eye on the afternoon soap operas. All of this and a great deal more can be had without your leaving the house. In the evening the movie theatres offer a variety of entertainment to choose from, including an interesting foreign film at an art theatre.

If you happen to live in a city where there is a legitimate theatre you may see a hit show, or your community or university theatre may be presenting a play—anything from Shakespeare to Shaw, from Molière to Arthur Miller.

Since the time of the ancient Greeks people have had theatre, but quantity of entertainment is our own twentieth-century contribution. However, the sources from which all the various forms of theatre stem can be found in the earliest plays ever written.

But long before men even learned to write, they were telling each other stories in terms of dramatic action. Imagine a scene among the early cave dwellers. People are sitting on rough logs. Winter is coming. Tribesmen have been out hunting. Suddenly in the distance triumphant cries are heard. The hunters return from the forest, great animals flung across their shoulders. They throw them down. They strut around the fire. The admiring onlookers say, "Ugh! Ugh!" (Or some such sound which means, "How did you kill such a big one?")

The chief hunter motions them all to be seated around the fire. He makes a little space for himself. He begins to pantomime. The onlookers strike their hands together to express their delight—the first applause. Here was the first theatre, here was the first audience.

Ever since that time, mankind has wanted to know the answers to the questions, "Where? When? Why? What? How?" And theatre has tried to give the answers.

Edith Hamilton, that loving friend of ancient Greece, describes in her book, *Mythology,* the sources of the myths which were the bases for so many Greek plays. Although she is speaking of historians and of classic poets, her comments show how individual the use of language must always be. Of Hesiod, the historian, she writes, "Hesiod is a notably simple writer . . . naïve, even childish, sometimes crude, always full of piety." These same qualities were evident in some of the successful plays of the eighties and nineties.

Miss Hamilton goes on to say, "The stories of classical mythology depend chiefly upon the Latin poet, Ovid." And she describes him as, "subtle, polished, artificial, self-conscious, and the complete sceptic." Do we not find similar qualities in, for example, Somerset Maugham's comedy, *Our Betters,* or in Noel Coward's farce, *Private Lives?*

Two thousand years' use of the written and spoken word has inevitably produced many changes in styles of writing. Much of the power and beauty of the ancient plays are lost in the process of translation. In the plays of Shakespeare there are words and idioms so unfamiliar to us that they might as well be in another language. Since Shakespeare's time English has undergone many changes. You really need a glossary of obsolete terms to understand some passages of his plays.

But long, long before Shakespeare, drama was flourishing in the Orient. The Indian classic, *Shakuntala,* was written in Sanskrit, reputedly in 400 A.D., by Kalidasa, the Shakespeare of India. It is a charming, tender story, told in lyric poetry. Stripped of the mystical trappings of ancient India and the poetry used in the telling of the story, you have the elements of a modern movie. It is the perennial tale of boy meets girl, girl loses boy—until, at long last, all problems are solved and boy and girl live happily ever after. The basic theme appeals to people in any country and in any time. There is a vivid account of this play and the production methods used in the theatre of Kalidasa in Sheldon Cheney's richly packed book, *The Theatre*. (I strongly recommend that you read this remarkable volume in its entirety.)

The Chinese theatre was and still is highly formalized, requiring actors trained from childhood in theatre techniques. The costumes used in Chinese plays have always been sumptuous to a degree seldom seen in our modern productions.

My own appearance in one ancient Chinese play revealed to me the delicate romance and the stern morality of early Chinese thought. *The Carefree Tree* is a thousand-year-old Chinese classic, which is still played in Peiping. It was produced at the Phoenix Theatre in New York as recently as 1955. Again, as in *Lysistrata* twenty-five hundred years ago in ancient Greece, the theme is a plea for the peaceful settling of the issues of war.

In the Chinese tradition, scenery may consist of a few chairs, some tables, some bamboo poles on which colored curtains are hung. A table may represent many different things: a mountain, a palace, or simply a table on which to write or place swords. Stools of different heights indicate mountains to be climbed. A soldier may pretend to commit suicide by jumping off a chair. The Chinese audience accepts the illusion.

A man in black strolls in and out of the play. He never speaks, he makes no gestures. He is the property man and he has numerous important functions to perform. He moves bits of scenery about, picks up a fan if the actor has dropped it; he discharges his duties in full view of the audience. It is assumed that he cannot be seen, and, strangely enough, he does become invisible because it is the Chinese tradition that he should be.

Stone tablets found in Egypt, Arabia, and Persia, show that drama with dialogue was part of the religious celebrations in the earliest temple ceremonies of the ancient world. In Athens some two thousand years ago these religious dramas, pagan in their content, preceded the plays of Aeschylus, Sophocles, Aristophanes, Euripides —plays which stand for all time as mountain peaks of literature.

Rome, after conquering Greece, replaced the classic Greek theatre with "the spectacle." Classic playwriting as an art disappeared. The Roman concept of entertainment, in contrast to the refinement and high morality of the Greek plays, became largely a savage exhibition of brute strength. Slaves and gladiators were forced to fight to the death in the arenas of Rome. Miniature naval battles, in which real ships and real weapons were used, provided some of the excitement. Christian victims thrown to the lions slaked the prevailing thirst for blood.

As the Roman Empire succumbed to increasing decay from within which eventually destroyed it, the Christian Church gradually took over. Slowly a new era emerged. Roman theatre continued to exist well into the sixth century A.D., but as the influence of the Christian Church grew more powerful, the decadent theatre of Rome withered away. In our sense of the word, theatre almost ceased to exist. A thousand years were to elapse before

9

the Church's influence brought it back to audiences of the Middle Ages.

But during the Dark Ages, strolling singers, acrobats, jugglers and minstrels wandered from town to town and from court to court, trading their tricks and their jokes for a square meal. Minstrelsy as an art found its expression in a new literature, in the *chansons* of the Middle Ages, in which dramatic stories were recounted or sung in the feudal castles of noble knights.

Then one day, sometime in the tenth century, during an Easter Mass, a priest said, *Quem quaeritis in sepulchre, Christocolae?* ("Whom seek ye in the sepulcher, followers of Christ?") Another priest answered the question in the scriptural words of Mary Magdalene. Dialogue was reborn.

This Easter Mass, called the *Quem Quaeritis* to this day, inspired similar treatment of other stories from the Bible. The priests recited their dialogue around the altar; then they added costumes. Theatre was looking up from its grave.

At first these plays or dialogues were devised and directed by priests of the Church. The common man was entranced. Here was diversion, an escape from the drab hardships of his daily life. At the courts the lords and their ladies had their own entertainment; their troubadours and their bards, who sang and improvised romantic tales of love and heroism. But for the peasants, the vassals, the Church supplied the only imaginative interest in the hard round of day-to-day living. The Church was not only their place of worship; it was their theatre, so to speak—their community center, their gathering place for contact with their fellows. It lent color to their dreary existence. So it is not surprising that before long these

Church dialogues emerged from the rituals of the services and began to be performed on the steps of the Church itself. These primitive efforts marked the beginnings of the religious Morality plays.

One of these early moralities was successfully revived by Max Reinhardt, the great German director, in the nineteen twenties. His production of *Everyman,* on the steps of the Cathedral in Salzburg, attracted the attention of theatre-goers all over the world. Here, every resource of lighting, of acting, and of staging was brought, for the first time in our day, to the service of a mediaeval religious play. Reinhardt made a memorable impact upon the imaginations of a highly sophisticated public.

But back in mediaeval times, in the civilized countries where literature was dormant, the Church dialogues expanded into more dramatic forms as the priests began to realize the value of employing the talents of the laity. The plays were simple or awe-inspiring, occasionally humorous. A stage direction in the *Mystery of Adam,* one of the earliest of the Mystery plays, instructs the actor playing Abel to put a saucepan under his shirt to protect himself from the knife blow that Cain gives him. This was no mere religious ceremony! Realism had made a tentative appearance.

Presently acrobats joined the ranks of the performers. The players began to make jokes about the Bible characters they were portraying. Mrs. Noah, for instance, became a gossip who chit-chatted with a friend while the men of her family struggled to lead the animals into the Ark. When the time for the departure of the Ark came she had to be pushed aboard like any donkey; the audience roared with delight.

By this time the workers' guilds had entered the picture. The bakers' guild, naturally, dramatized the story of Hell—a logical assignment, as who knew more about fires and ovens?

Performances began to be held at a regular hour. They began at four-thirty in the afternoon and lasted until sundown. Movable vans were hauled into the market place and around them a carnival-minded crowd would assemble. The actors had to exert themselves to put their plays across to their restless, noisy audiences. Gestures were bold, voices loud and clear, and lines such as these rang out sonorously:

> *I am gracious and great,*
> *God without beginning.*
> *I am Maker; I unmake;*
> *All might is in Me . . .*

The alliteration helped to carry the words to the crowding, straining listeners. Little by little the religious aspects and the direct references to Deity were trimmed away, until, by the sixteenth century, Morality plays as we know them had taken form.

Although religious characters still appeared in the plays, religious instruction as their prime objective was slowly giving way to entertainment. The early churchmen who, for the most part, devised the plots of these dramas, were not blind to the moral influence as well as the dramatic value of portraying hell-fire and damnation. Thus religious instruction and popular amusement were successfully combined.

Another step in progress occurred when, in 1547, at Valencienne in France, a Passion Play was presented on what was the first platform stage using a primitive suggestion of stage scenery.

But the development which brought back theatre in our sense of the word was the emergence in Italy of *Commedia dell' arte*. This style of presentation came into being not as formally written drama nor as "spectacle," in the Roman sense. The action of the *Commedia* plays took place on an almost bare platform, in the open air, and the actors used a minimum of props. The performers were skilled professionals; their dexterity of mind and body was acquired in the hard school of necessity—they must eat and live.

In Sheldon Cheney's book, *The Theatre,* we find this description of the *Commedia* players. "They strained their fancy to the utmost and improvised on the spot as their turn came and inspiration took them . . . They had only . . . to meet their stage manager in the morning . . . arrange the outline of the plot . . . hang the paper within easy reach of the wings; the rest they could invent themselves. They established a current between their audience and themselves out of which the mad farce rose, the joint product of them all."

These players were so knowledgeable in their craft, so amusing and so clever in weaving into their plots topics of local interest, that they kept their audiences in gales of laughter. One saw, when vaudeville was at its height, popular comedians like Frank Tinney, W. C. Fields, and Will Rogers doing exactly the same thing. Today, you catch an echo of this in the methods of Danny Kaye, Jack Benny, and others.

No two *Commedia* performances were quite alike.

Witty repartee was developed out of conventional gags, and slapstick "business" was a standard feature of the shows.

In the course of time groups of these players left their native Italy to infiltrate the theatres of France to such an extent that the French companies in Paris became jealous of the patronage which the visiting foreigners attracted and organized themselves in opposition. Some of the members of the *Commedia* companies became so successful that they bought theatres in Paris and settled into the life of the city.

The aristocrats began to attend the performances; even royalty patronized them. A stage-struck youngster named Jean Baptiste Poquelin hung around backstage as well as out front. This same youngster, a few years later, in 1643 to be exact, organized a group of amateurs, remodelled an old tennis court and the *Compagnie de Monsieur de Molière* was in business. The company was not a success in Paris and started touring the provinces. Molière's troupe spent twelve arduous years in barnstorming while their leader acted various parts, married his leading lady, and wrote plays. The little company was learning "the business." These years of apprenticeship were invaluable. Out of them Molière distilled not only a familiarity with audience reaction, but a seasoned philosophy of life and human nature which served him well in his maturity as a playwright. Those early years of seeming failure were a blessing in disguise.

It is amazing how history repeats itself. Four hundred years later, in Russia, a group of amateurs joined forces under the guidance of Constantin Stanislavsky, a wealthy enthusiast in the arts, and created in 1898 what became the world-famous Moscow Art Theatre. Something similar occurred when some ambitious amateurs in the United States banded together (in 1915-16) to form the Washington Square Players. Beginning in the tiny bandbox theatre on the East Side of New York, they produced unusual, "artistic" plays, gradually growing in experience and winning a loyal following. Later, they changed their name to The Theatre Guild, an organization which, as everyone knows, has made theatre history.

In Paris Molière began producing sparkling, sophisticated comedies that the world acknowledges as the finest of their kind.

Under his aegis the art of delicate word-play was enjoyed in candlelighted jewel-box theatres, where the ability to destroy a reputation with a well-turned phrase indicated high breeding and vastly amused the worldlings who made up the audiences. Polite drawingroom comedies were performed with a precision of style worthy of a minuet or a duel. Intrigue was the order of the day, both on and off the stage.

In France in the early eighteenth century Adrienne Lecouvreur, whose personal life was quite as dramatic as any she portrayed on the stage, became a reigning favorite. Her naturalism was a departure from the stilted grandiloquence of her contemporary rivals. The change in the style of acting which she introduced found full expression in England in the illustrious career of David Garrick.

Garrick, who entered upon the London theatre scene in 1740, became one of the finest as well as one of the most popular actors of any period. As a star and manager of the Drury Lane Theatre, he found time, despite his exacting duties, to write some forty-odd plays. They have not survived as literature and are almost never revived.

15

Even before Garrick's day, in England a man named William Congreve was using the same polished technique made popular by Molière. As in France, emotions wore masks. Sincerity was démodé.

All this was changed by the French Revolution.

As we enter the nineteenth century we find that theatre-going had become an accepted part of modern life. By then "vehicles" were being designed primarily to exploit the particular talents and personalities of popular stars.

With the Victorian age came plays that were for the most part prudish in treatment. Particularly in England many subjects were tabu. There was a kind of hothouse atmosphere which precluded the presentation of controversial ideas. To be genteel, well-bred—above all to be a "lady" or a "gentleman"—was the primary requisite of a successful actor.

Suddenly, in the late nineteenth century, into this over-heated climate of the theatre there came, like a cold, cleansing wind, a genius whose courageous tackling of forbidden subjects altered the whole pattern of playwriting. There was no synthetic glamour in the plays of Henrik Ibsen. Prettiness, false sentiment, melodramatic clichés, were blown sky-high before the uncompromising honesty and the superb craftsmanship of Ibsen's plays.

Beginning as a stage manager in a provincial theatre in Norway, Ibsen became the catalyst responsible for most of the vitality of our modern theatre. In the Victorian theatre certain things were not done, in any case not talked about! But this little giant of the North opened up sealed closets, dragged out skeletons and plunked them right into the laps of a horrified public. One simply did not discuss such subjects as Ibsen presented: syphilis, civic dishonesty, women who justified the abandonment of husband and children. And how could Victorian audiences be expected to accept as a heroine a really disagreeable woman named Hedda Gabler who kills herself in sheer distaste for life? Yet it is she who has survived all the sugary heroines of the popular plays of those days. In our own time we have met her in Lillian Hellman's *The Little Foxes;* in *Craig's Wife* by George Kelly; in Louis Anspacher's play, *The Unchastened Woman.* Poor Hedda, who so loathed the idea of maternity, has spawned a whole theatreful of heroines.

Ibsen made the stage every man's living room and most people did not always like what they saw there. He dealt constructively with social problems of his day and age. He freed whole generations from the restrictions of conventional morality and proved that real people, even when no larger than life-size, are dramatic material of tremendous power. He brought realism into the theatre and his followers are legion.

While all this had been taking place in Europe, in America theatre was mushrooming. The seventeenth-century Puritans had done their utmost to eliminate theatre, but performances constantly sprang up in spite of the harshest social disapproval. By 1778 theatre was so well established that George Washington was able to see a play at Valley Forge. Some half-century or so later, a little creature named Lotta Crabtree became the idol of the gold miners in the Far West. When she danced and sang her topical songs their enthusiasm was unbounded and they threw bags of gold dust onto the stage. They literally worshipped her and her beguiling charms.

In the last two decades of the nineteenth century the population of the country had doubled. Every town of any importance had its "opery" house and stock and traveling companies played to packed houses. Two thousand stock companies provided priceless opportunities for young actors to learn their craft the hard way. Some did as many as ten to fourteen performances every week.

Even many decades later remnants of this grueling routine still existed. I sometimes shudder to remember that very early in my own career, when I was avidly seizing upon any and every opportunity to gain experience in important parts, I once played a fourteen-week engagement with the Poli Stock Company in New Haven, Connecticut, where I did daily matinees as well as seven evening performances! We rehearsed every morning from ten to one, with the exception of Thursday morning when we were graciously permitted to stay at home until noon so that we might memorize our lines for the next show.

During the era of Edwin Booth, in the second half of the last century, stars such as he were expected to perform in several different plays a week. Supporting players were permanent members of the local companies whose chief acting assignment was to learn what positions to take in relation to the star. Traveling conditions were deplorable. Yet from this system some of our greatest actors and actresses emerged.

The tastes of the public were simple. Millions delighted in the burnt-cork antics of *Lew Dockstader's Magnificent Minstrels*. Vaudeville circuits flourished. Burlesque had its special audiences from coast to coast. Circuses traveling from Podunk to Broadway thrilled spectators of all ages. P. T. Barnum opened his Museum in 1842 in New York where he exhibited freaks, natural history curiosities, and also imported from Europe, to sing at the famous Castle Garden at the Battery, one of the greatest sopranos of her day, Miss Jenny Lind.

Managers like Augustin Daly and Lester Wallack established very high standards of production and of acting in the theatres called by their names. Road stars like Clara Morris and, later, Otis Skinner bent all their efforts to become regular members of these aristocratic institutions of the theatre. The classics as well as new plays by currently popular playwrights were well patronized and the theatre of "ladies and gentlemen" basked in the glamour of champagne and candlelight. In 1907 Ziegfeld's first *Follies* opened, providing an eager public with the opportunity of gazing at hundreds of beautiful girls whose lovely forms, scantily covered in sequins, ostrich feathers, *et al.*, were displayed against incredibly lavish backdrops. With these shows Flo Ziegfeld introduced Glamour with a capital "G."

"Entertainment" still meant, for the most part, "live" performances, although some odd contraptions called nickelodeons were making furtive appearances in obscure neighborhoods.

The whole world was holiday-minded and its mood was vividly reflected in the theatre. A kind of happy innocence marked those years of our country's growth. But in 1914 that world ended with a crash. World War I was upon us.

In the period between two world wars, plays and pictures began to reflect life in a very different key. The drama of social significance appeared; playwrights like John Howard Lawson, Eugene O'Neill, and Clifford

Odets began to be heard from. The under dog became a hero. Robert Sherriff's war play, *Journey's End,* the entire action of which took place in a dugout behind the lines, with a cast made up solely of men, created a powerful impression upon audiences on both sides of the Atlantic. Laurence Stallings' and Maxwell Anderson's *What Price Glory?* was a lusty, sardonic commentary on the conduct of the doughboy.

Since those days, legitimate theatre, movies, radio, television, have all expanded beyond the wildest dreams of actors and audiences of the past. Whereas theatres originally held audiences ranging in size from fifty to a hundred people in the small houses and up to a thousand people and over in the larger ones, today a single performance of a play on TV may attract millions.

Who can tell what may come next? Millions of dollars are spent in producing today's shows. Any moment may introduce a new technique, a new idea, a new style of production. But in comedy or tragedy, in modern or period plays, there is nothing newer than ancient history. The program you see tonight on TV may be based on a Greek play of two thousand years ago. It may be written in the manner of an Elizabethan masterpiece or it may be performed in the manner of a Chinese drama. It may even be styled after the Japanese or Hindu theatre.

Look closely and you may see the family resemblance.

What Makes Thespis Tick?

GREAT SHOW! Terrific reviews! But why is it good? What's the show about? Here's a simple test: if you can answer me in a few sentences without naming names or describing characters, and if your few sentences make a clear, understandable story, then you've seen a good play.

If you can't, if you have to go into a long description of each character, relating episode after episode, detail after detail, if there is no over-all idea that stays with you, then you've seen a play that will be here today and gone tomorrow; that may be remembered as long as you can remember the plot; that may possibly be recalled only for the skills of the actors who played in it.

Take the time-honored story of *Romeo and Juliet*, trim it right down to the basic plot. A boy and a girl, born of feuding families, meet and fall in love. Because of the feud they cannot marry. So a simple though dangerous plan is devised. Juliet takes a sleeping potion that will make her appear to die just at the time her family has arranged for her marriage to another suitor. Romeo finds her lying in the family burial vault and, believing her dead, kills himself. When Juliet awakens she finds his body beside her. Using his dagger, she stabs herself.

Stripped down to its bare bones, this is the plot.

Even greater simplification is possible. If anyone asks you what *Romeo and Juliet* is about, you can either tell them the whole story, or you can simply say, "Love is more important than race, creed, or family feuds."

This message, this theme, is timeless and universal. It was used in Shakespeare's sixteenth century, it is used today, and it will probably be in use five hundred years from now. The love of individuals in conflict with prejudices and hostilities is a basic human situation. The theme constantly appears in the twentieth century. We find it in Anne Nichols' *Abie's Irish Rose,* in which the lovers struggle not against families, but against religious prejudices, Catholic and Jewish. In musical form the theme is repeated in *West Side Story.* In this modern Romeo plot the lovers are in conflict with the hatreds of two rival street gangs.

In all these examples the theme will be remembered long after plot details are forgotten. You may not recall just how Juliet obtained the sleeping potion or how Romeo and Juliet first met, but you will remember that it was the unreasoning hatred of two families that caused the death of their children. The tragic irony will remain with you. You will find yourself referring to this story as long as you live. Your decisions and your viewpoint will be more humane and understanding for having that story somewhere in your consciousness.

It doesn't matter that Juliet was an Italian girl of fourteen who may or may not have been old enough to marry. It doesn't matter that Romeo had no visible means of supporting her. Those non-essentials are mere plot details. The theme itself cannot become dated; it cannot become the exclusive property of any one group, for the reason that it concerns human nature which changes very little no matter how great the passage of time.

Chinese, Greek, English, Indian theatre all seem to have borrowed from each other—to be related. And why? Because they all are concerned with the same basic subject, human nature.

A Western is not only a play about a good sheriff who wins and a bad man who loses, set in a desert town and showing us a field of galloping horses. If it runs true to form, the play says quite simply that virtue and goodness have the elements of strength and so will triumph. This fundamental conflict has appealed to people since time and story-making began. The right wins. The good man triumphs. The gangster perishes and the FBI man gets the girl and a promotion. The scene may be today's West Side New York, the American Civil War, or Renaissance Italy. The setting is unimportant and temporary. The theme is important and permanent.

There are really only a few basic stories that are rewritten to suit each generation. The trimmings are altered to fit the times, but the essential themes remain the same. You can find the same play in a dozen languages in as many centuries.

Obviously, an author cannot just sit down at his typewriter with a theme in mind and dash off a play. He must have a story to tell and the story must contain some struggle or conflict. It must have in it something you wish to see happen and something you don't. Because you *must care* about the way things turn out. Your hero may be wading through one hilarious blunder after another (as might Jerry Lewis, for instance), or he may be outwitting a band of cutthroat crooks determined to do him in. Whether it is humor or horror, you must have a hero or a heroine. There must be "someone to root for," as a famous theatrical producer once put it. What represents "the right" may be an individual or a group. Your hero may be blond and handsome, or a crotchety old man with the charm of a Barry Fitzgerald or an Edmund Gwenn. The villain may be a sinister fellow with a black mustache, or "the wrong" may be embodied in the respectable members of a large corporation. Trappings, costumes, characterizations—all these vary of course, but today more than ever before it is the conflict that matters. The opposing forces as they affect your emotions are the essential.

Whatever the plot, the characters must somehow be believable. They may even be inconsistent in their behavior *if* the author can make you believe that they had to be that way. It takes more than a dark mustache and a sinister leer to make a villain; more than good looks to make a hero. Characters must be real—must seem to be

24

following genuine impulses. This doesn't mean that they have to behave as you and I do, but as we *might* behave, given their personalities, their circumstances. What they say must ring true. The dialogue need not necessarily duplicate a conversation you might overhear on a street corner, but it must seem natural speech for the characters to be using. Then it will ring true. Moreover, it must ring true in the vernacular of whatever period the author is writing about.

All this doesn't just happen. A play doesn't, like Topsy, "jes' grow." Given a story and a conflict, believable characters saying believable things, the playwright must still struggle with his material. He must immediately capture your interest and hold it. He must keep you in suspense and involve you in the problems of his characters until the final curtain or the fade-out on the screen.

His play must be more than a mere series of incidents. If this were not true he could simply sit in a railroad station, taking down what he sees and hears—and, presto!, he would have a play. But he would not have a play. This is not to say that he could not find dramatic material in a railroad station—enough for a dozen comedies and just as many tragedies. But without dramatic structure he would no more have a play than you could put over a funny story by using the punch line first. He must introduce his characters, unfold his plot, provide suspense, reach a climax, and bring everything to a conclusion that you can accept as inevitable.

After writing the above I happened upon some comments in an article by Brooks Atkinson, drama critic of *The New York Times,* that sheds the light of his lambent prose upon this very subject. Speaking of a playwright's unsuccessful attempt to fashion a play about a famous

25

actor of another day, Mr. Atkinson said, "He [the playwright] seems to have no point of view. His prose is routine and tasteless and makes a colorful character uninteresting. Blanche Du Bois was a colorless person, but in *A Streetcar Named Desire* she became a memorable figure—lost and lonely—because Tennessee Williams can create beauty by the use of words. Willie Loman was a dull man. He acquired heroic stature in *Death of A Salesman* because Arthur Miller writes prose with vigor and insight. By the use of words he can dramatically define an obscure man's position in relation to the universe.

"In a play words seem to express the thoughts of the characters . . . but ultimately what they express is the mind and spirit of the author. If he uses words with force and originality he can make the most unlikely material come alive in the theatre; and no matter what his subject may be or who his characters are, the play bears his personal image. For words are the only means he has for proving that he is . . . a writer. The most stimulating plays need not be those with the most stimulating themes or characters. They are the plays that glow with the author's personality. . . . The playwright is not a recording machine. He is interested in all sorts of people, and if he has talent he writes about them with originality."

If a playwright has an important idea to present or a significant comment to make—and has learned his craft—his play may stand a chance of becoming "a classic." (A classic simply means that what the author says continues to interest audiences for a long, long time.) If he has only a well-built story of topical interest, his play may be merely a box-office success. And goodness knows no one objects to that! Many playwrights would settle for it. (Most managers would too.)

26

All this I have been talking about forms the basic design for a play, but the manner in which this basic design is handled varies tremendously.

Let's look for a minute at the problems of the writer for television. He must consider the limitations of his screen—which may measure no more than twenty-one inches in your living room. It is obviously impossible for him to use too many actors at one time for if he does so the story action may be lost in a crowd of tiny moving figures.

This particular limitation was very obvious in an adaptation for television of Dickens' *A Tale of Two Cities*, where the scene showing the storming of the Bastille became a blur of confused crowds in action. On the wider screens used in motion pictures, such condensation is not necessary. In the film version of the same story, the Bastille sequence was one of the most telling in the picture.

Apart from the restrictions imposed by the size of his screen, the playwright for television has still other problems to solve. There is little time for exposition. Take, for example, the popular *Dragnet* show in which Jack Webb plays Joe Friday. He begins by saying bluntly, "My name is Joe Friday. On the sixteenth of January it was cold in Los Angeles. We got a phone call. . . ." And then he starts to let you in on what and whom the detectives are after. This is a frank, direct admission of the necessity for exposition. He says, in effect, "Let me give you the facts and then we can get on with the story." In a way, this is quite unrealistic drama, as you can see. Jack Webb, alias Joe Friday, steps out of the framework of the story in order to talk directly to you in the audience. You, the television viewer, accept this convention—which is really quite surprising when you come to think about it, for so often George Q. Public resents soliloquies and "asides" in some of the so-called classics.

This same direct exposition technique appears again and again throughout theatre history. It was used more than six centuries ago by a Chinese playwright in a drama called *The Chalk Circle*. In it Mrs. Ch'ang opens the play by saying, "I am a native of Ch'ing Ch'ao. My family name was Liu; that of my husband was Ch'ang. He died very young, a long time ago, and left me two children." And so on. It's a long way from Mrs. Ch'ang to Joe Friday, but the device is the same.

Motion pictures create still a different problem for the playwright. What do the larger-than-life-size figures and the intimate realism of the movie camera impose upon his techniques? The movies have created a whole new style of dialogue—terse understatement is the order of the day because the camera makes it possible to tell so much by purely visual means.

In the days of David Belasco, whose active producing career ran well into the nineteen thirties, photographic realism on the stage reached its peak. Belasco would furnish a room down to its most minute detail. If he were showing you a woodland scene, the running brook would be real water. If actors were to dine on the stage, the meal would consist of highly edible food properly served. His wizardry in the creation of lighting was almost incredible. With it he achieved illusions of unimagined realism. I remember one effect in Eugene Walter's play, *The Easiest Way*, which Belasco produced. The first-act setting showed the veranda of a luxurious resort hotel in Colorado. In the background one saw snow-capped mountains. The scene progressed from late afternoon into twilight. As the shadows grew deeper the changing colors on the mountaintops were so beautifully modulated, all light finally being pinpointed to the glow of one cigarette, that the absorbed audience broke into enchanted applause as the curtain fell on darkness.

These lighting miracles were no accident. Belasco kept an inventive master electrician under permanent contract. All year round, and often late into the small hours, these two indefatigable workers would experiment with the marvelous "juice" supplied by another wizard, Thomas Edison. Many of the most important progressive steps in theatre lighting can be traced back to the experiments of these two men.

But in Europe in the early nineteen hundreds, new concepts were beginning to make their influence felt. Adolph Appia and Gordon Craig designed stage settings of breath-taking beauty. They inspired experiments which swept out of the theatre much of the overly realistic scenery which had cluttered the world stages for so many decades. They made use of great architectural masses; lighting was their chief instrument. Their vision was never fully realized in the popular commercial theatre. But the influence of these men was far-reaching. They opened the way for artists like Robert Edmond Jones, Norman Bel Geddes, and Lee Simonson in America; Jacques Copeau and Charles Dullin in France; Leopold Jessner and Max Reinhardt in Germany.

In America it was in the Arthur Hopkins productions of *The Jest, Richard III,* and *Hamlet,* all three starring John Barrymore, that Robert Edmond Jones made fullest use of the new concepts. These same influences can be seen in the theatre of today in the stage designs of Jo Mielziner and many of his contemporaries. Lee Simonson, in his book, *The Stage Is Set*, has given us a vivid and illuminating picture of the evolution of stage design. (The book is a vastly entertaining one, quite apart from its informative value, by the way.)

Simplification was carried even further, with refreshing results, in the production of Thornton Wilder's *Our Town*. This, you remember, is the story of plain people in an American village. They were not big or important people. Their emotions—love and sorrow, their lives, their marriages and births and deaths—were what Wilder made us care about. Had he put his characters in realistic settings—shown us a garden wall, a New England cottage filled with furniture, a fully equipped drugstore—we would have been distracted from the simple outline of the story. But because of the mere suggestions of settings used in the original production, one's imagination was vividly engaged. A plank laid across two chairs became a drugstore counter; a stepladder represented a stairway. Audiences were moved by emotions that are familiar to us all. The life of the whole village unfolded; the street corners, the railroad station, the cemetery in a downpour of rain—one saw them all.

Shakespeare makes an even greater challenge to our imagination. His scenery was painted in words. (The success of John Gielgud's program of Shakespeare readings, *The Ages of Man,* which the famous contemporary English actor presented in many parts of the world, reminds us once again how vivid those word pictures can be.) The theatre of Shakespeare's day involved him in still other problems. His stage was little more than a platform where actors performed in the sunlight. Elizabethan audiences created with their own imaginations the illusion of time and place.

In Shakespeare's day, the playwright was under no constraint to make his characters or his situations conform to contemporary standards of behavior. Human as his characters were, common as were the impulses he dealt with, they were still larger than life. Nobody expected to meet Macbeth walking down the street or to watch Lady Macbeth trying on a wimple. There are few real-life people, nor were there many even in those days, who would stop in mid-action to poetically describe the moonlight or the surrounding forest scene. To do so was an accepted convention at that time—as acceptable to the Elizabethan audiences as are our TV commercials today.

The Greeks also worked without realistic settings or properties. Their plays were done in enormous amphitheatres under the open sky. Naturally, gestures had to be broad and sweeping. Speeches were long and voices magnificently trained for their carrying power. The masks the actors wore were designed to convey facial expressions across the wide spaces of the outdoor auditoriums, and the players stood on high-soled shoes, called *cothurns*, which were sometimes ten inches high. This naturally gave them imposing stature. Realism was neither desirable nor was it possible. Everything—characterizations, speeches, the plots themselves—were of epic proportions; the plays as well as the vast theatres required this.

In my own experience, when I revived Sophocles' *Electra* in a Broadway theatre in New York, I had occasion to realize very keenly the relationship between style of writing, the dramatic concept, and the background against which the drama would be played. All the actors in the cast felt cramped. Beautiful as was the setting designed by the late James Reynolds, there was simply not space enough for the type of play we were trying to do.

Later, when I did *Electra* in the open-air Greek Theatre in Berkeley, California, the entire play became more powerful, more moving, and grander in scale in the broad surroundings that were so similar to those in which the play had been presented to the audiences of Athens two thousand years ago. The Berkeley setting consisted of the back wall of the eighty-foot-wide stage, broken by three doors. The center door, through which the principal actors passed, was about thirty feet high; on either side were doors half as high which were used by the chorus for its entrances and exits. The high central doors were of simulated bronze. The illusion of their tremendous weight was created by two husky students (probably stage-struck football heroes) who, made up as almost-nude Nubian slaves, pushed these doors with seemingly great effort each time the Queen made an entrance or an exit.

Such was the stage setting for the story of Electra, the daughter of the murdered King Agamemnon. She had refused to accept as king Aegisthos, her mother's accomplice in the murder of her father, Agamemnon. For years Electra had nursed her solitary hatred while waiting for the return of her brother, Orestes, whose responsibility it was to avenge his father's murder.

It is a massive story. To set it in less than massive simplicity reduces the impact of this wonderful drama.

Toward the end of the play Orestes returns to the place of his birth to fulfill his dedicated purpose. He enters the palace and kills the Queen. His mother's dead body is brought in on a bier over which has been cast an immense crimson covering.

As we staged this scene, when the body was uncovered for the King to see, the long red cloth was cast away in such a movement as to make it ripple down the steps leading to the circle where stood the altar with its votive offerings. Electra, crouched at the foot of these steps, watched Orestes force the King, at sword's point, back into the palace, there to meet his fate in the same spot where he had killed Agamemnon. A death cry was heard from within, then silence. In the breathless pause that followed, Electra, still crouching—tense, alone—realized that clutched in her hands was the royal crimson covering which had concealed the body of her dead mother. Slowly she rose, mesmerized by the symbol of power she was holding in her hands. Rising to her full height, she laid the richly colored stuff across her shoulders. Moving slowly up the steps, she crossed the deep stage to the great bronze doors, the long trail of red following in her wake. As she reached the doors she stepped into a pool of golden light, and majestically reentered, in silence, her father's palace. The red scarf slowly trailing behind her was the last moving thing seen as the lights blacked out.

The effect was electric. Never have I seen so excited an audience. Stage direction can heighten the effectiveness of even a masterpiece.

Greek audiences were familiar with what was going to happen. They knew the plots of the legendary stories as well as they knew their own life histories. Audiences of today are frequently in the same position.

One's interest and pleasure in a familiar story are of a special kind. One looks for new values which an actor may have discovered. Who goes to see *Hamlet* with any curiosity about the story? You want to see what the new actor brings to the part.

It is easy to stumble over a speech written in archaic language, with unfamiliar references, easy to be confused by unfamiliar conventions. But the curious soul (and I am hoping that you are one) will push on farther to find the characterizations behind the words, the ideas woven into the plot, the soul of man revealed behind the ideas. All these are part of the fabric of the great dramas of the ages. For these plays have endured for a good reason—because time cannot wear out their truth and their power.

They Teach Us to Laugh

A<small>LL THE WORLD</small> loves a lover?" All the world loves a comedian. We give him the affection of our hearts and the money from our pockets. In return he gives us the priceless gift of laughter.

How dull life would be without him and his humor! Learning would be bone-dry, self-criticism almost impossible. He makes us laugh, sometimes at each other, often at ourselves. Comedy means laughter and laughter means a good time. So at least half of the theatre you watch, half of the entertainment offered you, is probably comedy, or at least an attempt at comedy.

Comedy includes everything from the antics of a clown to the subtlest, most wry comments on human nature.

Consider the hundreds of things that make you laugh. You laugh at funny faces and at dead-pan ones, at clowns, at inconsecutive chatterboxes like Gracie Allen, at the fat man who insists on wearing a coat that is too small and then splits his pants. In the movies you have laughed at the custard pie thrown in the actor's face; you laugh when a man slips on a banana peel, or when a chair is pulled out from under him. You laugh at punctured pomposity. A child laughs instinctively when an angry father spills milk on the tablecloth. But a clever playwright finds more subtle ways to make you laugh.

In *Peg O' My Heart,* the Hartley Manners play in which his wife, Laurette Taylor, starred for so many years, little Irish Peg finds herself in the midst of a snobbish family of English aristocrats. Her simple honesty, her frank Irish wit, puncture all their pretensions and their plans to take advantage of her are reduced to rubble.

Even before *Peg,* this pattern was very popular with play-goers some forty years ago. The honest homespun American was always getting the better of sophisticated "foreigners." William Hodge in *The Man From Home,* a dramatization of one of Booth Tarkington's most popular books, is a fine example of this type of comedy. Nowadays life seems less simple, in the theatre as well as in real life. Yet we still laugh at complications which arise from the contrasts in the *mores* of different nationalities. Mistaken identity is a sure-fire subject for laughter. We laugh at puns, at jokes, at limericks, even at witticisms which have barbs in them. Much laughter is based on cruelty; most satire certainly is. I would almost go so far as to say that satire is bound to be cruel. Just watch the face of someone whose mannerisms are being caricatured for the delight of an audience. The victim may say gaily, "How clever! How amusing!" But there is mayhem in his heart.

Edward G. Robinson, in an interview with columnist Louis Sobol, expressed himself on this subject. Said Robinson, "I have the plot all set for my next picture. I line up all the mimics who do impressions of me against a wall and shoot them down with a machine gun."

I ran across a really illuminating summary of satire in a newspaper article by Howard Teichmann, co-author of the hit comedy, *The Solid Gold Cadillac*. He said, in part, "The Romans were the first to use the word satire. . . . What it was then and what it is now are not particularly far apart. As one of the capital divisions of literature, satire in its essence is the criticism of man and his works, holding up either or both to ridicule or scorn. As a work, satire differs from comedy, farce, or burlesque in that it has a point of view. Whatever it goes after it attempts to expose, and, if possible, to fix responsibility. It may concern itself with politics, economics, morals or manners. It may be biting, pungent, severe or ironic. But without humor satire descends to invective. . . . The Romans . . . with biting sarcasm . . . trenchant wit, keenness and caricature, made it into a laughing literary lash."

Satire is not always bitter. In Garson Kanin's *Born Yesterday*, the "beautiful but dumb" blonde was satirized with affectionate understanding and played with infinite charm by Judy Holliday.

There is laughter in the wrong word used in the right

place, as when Mrs. Malaprop in Richard Brinsley Sheridan's *The Rivals* voices her famous theories on the subject of education: "I would by no means wish a daughter of mine to be a progeny of learning. I don't think so much learning becomes a young woman. Nor would I wish her to meddle with . . . the more inflammatory branches of learning. . . . I would have her instructed in geometry so that she might know something of the contagious countries, etc., etc. . . ." The malapropisms of this famous character have continued to enchant audiences ever since they were first uttered on a London stage in 1775.

Who has not laughed at someone else's malapropisms? Behind our laughter there is apt to be a sense of superiority. Then too, there is a kind of laughter based on hysteria. You laugh nervously when a public speaker stutters helplessly, or when an actor, making a tragic exit, stumbles on a stairway. You laugh from sheer embarrassment when an unfortunate actress loses her petticoat on stage. You cannot imagine the untold agony of the player at such moments as these. I once had to cross the stage, inch by inch, praying that the skirt which I was clutching around me with my upstage hand would not fall about my ankles until I had reached the exit.

A great playwright can even make you laugh at humor in the midst of tragedy. Read the last act of Ibsen's *The Wild Duck,* in which little Hedwig's father returns home after a night of carousing, petulantly insisting on being given his breakfast while making grandiose plans to leave the house forever. During this scene, deliberately written for laughs, the audience is waiting to hear the shot from the garret off-stage into which Hedwig has crept to kill herself.

Ibsen not only destroyed the conventional formulas of playwriting but he interlarded his serious plays with wry and perceptive humor which all too often is lost in the English translations. His comments on human foibles are the very essence of comedy. He put new wine into old bottles.

The great Russian, Anton Chekhov, went even further. He threw the bottles out of the window.

Chekhov claimed that all his plays were comedies. Examine the pattern of *The Sea Gull* and *The Cherry Orchard.* Futile elements of society are pitilessly shown for what they are. Chekhov's characters are depicted as part of a provincial society in the Russia of the late eighties which was bogged down in inefficiency and hopelessness. That these people existed not only in Russia but in our own country was shown when Joshua Logan adapted *The Cherry Orchard,* putting the story into a setting in the American South and calling it *The Wisteria Trees.*

Chekhov did not attempt to make things happen. He was, in fact, more concerned with things that did not happen. It is a little as if he invited us to creep up to an open window in order to overhear bits of conversation by means of which his characters carry on the business of their lives. No pattern of action seems to be moving them. But these fragments of conversation gradually reveal constraints, inner tensions, emotional stresses and frustrated desires, which move us far more than could any melodramatic story.

These plays seemingly have no beginning, no end, only a middle. They are slices of life. Chekhov's characters drift in and out of the scene. A chance remark or a scrap of dialogue may seem to be all that you are hearing. But gradually you come to know more about these people

39

than you know about those who surround you in your daily life. He shows you with rueful humor how absurd their aspirations are, how pitiful their wishful thinking. But it is his compassionate understanding, his sympathy with his unheroic heroes and heroines, if indeed you can call them that, which make Chekhov's plays what they are —masterpieces painted on a small canvas.

George Bernard Shaw could twist words and make paradoxical statements so cleverly and so amusingly that audiences laugh at ideas which in themselves are anything but laughable. It was his way of making them listen and remember his ideas the better because of the laughter. In *The Doctor's Dilemma*, he has written a death scene in which a patient dying of tuberculosis mercilessly spoofs his doctors and the whole medical profession. He finally makes a brilliant paraphrase of the Christian creed and dies in full view of the audience. From a theatrical viewpoint the scene is more poignant, the message of the play more effective, just because Shaw uses comedy in the midst of sadness.

Basically, there are three kinds of comedy—that of character, of incident, and of dialogue. Some comedies include all three; some more of one type than the other. These three range from elementary slapstick to extremely polished and highly developed comedy. Pie-slinging belongs at the lowest rung of the comedy-of-incident ladder. Oscar Wilde's play, *The Importance of Being Earnest*, has scintillating, satirical word-play. Comedy of dialogue ranges all the way from the current comedy of insult so popular on many of our television programs, to Sir James Barrie's exquisite whimsey.

We have rules for laughter, both on stage and off. There are some funny things you don't laugh at. Only a child or a boor is likely to laugh at old age or infirmity. Some people laugh because they are too insensitive to realize that their laughter will hurt. All of this a first-rate playwright knows by instinct and he shapes his material accordingly.

The less civilized a person or a society is, the less taste and appreciation is there for the comedy of ideas and the more elementary is the kind of comedy enjoyed. In less complicated societies than our own, audiences did laugh uproariously at someone's misfortunes. The Elizabethans used to laugh at Shylock, even though Shakespeare built him as a tragic character, which of course is the way he is played in our own time.

Comedy itself is always basically the same, but audiences have changed. In comparison with our Greek ancestors, we are fairly restrained and civilized. The banana-peel incident that you may have seen on television would have had to be infinitely more vulgar to have wowed them in Athens two thousand years ago. I have been shocked at some of the obscenities used for comic effect in some of the less well-known farces of the ancient Greeks. The Greeks indulged in sexual jokes and in physical "pieces of business," as we call it professionally, which simply would not be tolerated today.

You will recall that in our quick review of theatre history we talked about *Commedia dell' arte* as a milestone in the development of the theatre. *Commedia dell' arte* emerged from the Dark Ages, a period when life was too grim for much laughter. But people are born with funny-bones whether they use them or not. Out of the need to laugh there developed, around the fifteenth century, a style of humor which satisfied this need. Wandering players banded together, improvised little plays about boy meets girl, boy gets girl, boy loses girl, and other stories not too different from the subjects we enjoy today. Comedians like Danny Kaye, Jerry Lewis, W. C. Fields, Charlie Chaplin, have done and do many of the things that were the backbone of *Commedia dell' arte*.

Let's have a closer look at this *Commedia* business. The time is about 1570. We are in Italy—a sunny country where people love to stroll about and enjoy the out-of-doors—the right climate for laughter. A drum booms in the distance. People gather in groups to see the parade of players who have come to town, much as we watch the arrival of the circus. Of course you have stood on the curb watching the circus come to town, delighting in the elephants, the clowns, and the lovely ladies on horseback. But this *Commedia dell' arte* troupe has no elephants, no prancing white horses, no great tent. Usually it has only a wagon drawn by a donkey, a few bits of portable scenery, and some trunks for costumes.

These costumes are important. They are the labels by which you identify the players. That worn by Harlequin is made of many-colored diamond-shaped patches; Pantaloon may have ruffles, and he wears a long false nose. He usually carries a prop consisting of two wooden sticks with which he makes a spanking noise as he slaps them, usually against some one's posterior. This was always good for a laugh and gave us the word which is used nowadays

to describe the broadest, the most obvious kind of comedy
—"slapstick." A stock of reliable jokes was used repeatedly. In vaudeville in its early days we used to hear similar ones.

"Who was that lady I saw you with?" "That wasn't no lady, that was my wife," is a moss-grown classic.

Each member of the *Commedia* troupe played his own particular character, his "line," as theatre people call it. Columbine was the leading lady, always pursued by the men who desired her, always young and prettily dressed. Harlequin, in the course of time, underwent several changes. At first a kind of stupid buffoon, a tool of the other actors, he became, through the brilliant talent of the famous clown, Biancolleli (circa 1695), a witty, sophisticated fellow, capable of much mischief.

Pantaloon and Scaramouche were the character comics. Pierrot evolved from a somewhat stupid type into a symbol of unrequited love, the lover who is full of tenderness and longing but who always loses his girl. (He is not unlike Hamlet.) Part of the appeal of this character lies in the traditional appearance he presents—the dead-white face with its sorrowful eyes, the black skull cap framing it, the white ruff and loose jacket with its row of pom-poms down the front, and the wide, flapping pantaloons. Do look him up; for me he has irresistible charm.

Actually, what was done in those days was very much like the casting of parts in the stock companies of fifty years ago and later, in our own country, when actors were engaged to do a certain "line" of parts for which their personalities and appearances suited them. In those early stock companies an actor was engaged for "romantic leads," for "second business" (which meant the secondary parts), for "juveniles," for "heavies," or for comics. The lowest paid members of the company were listed as "general utility." These various types appeared in many different kinds of plays, serious as well as comic, and many of our finest leading players got their experience in such companies.

Through the years *Commedia* grew in quality and importance so that the *Commedia* troupes ventured into other countries beside their native Italy. The Italian players were soon installed in Paris at the *Hôtel de Bourgogne*. In the soil of these comic plays France's greatest comic genius was nurtured. Molière recreated many of the stock *Commedia* characters, but from them he built up recognizable human beings.

He lashed out against sham of all kinds. In *L'Avare* he satirizes miserliness; in *Les Femmes Savantes* ("The Learned Ladies") he makes fun of the intellectual pretensions of the "blue-stockings" at Court. *Le Bourgeois Gentilhomme* ("The Would-Be Gentleman") ridicules social climbers, snobs, those who feel they must "keep up with the Joneses." Our own beloved Bobby Clark enchanted his public in this play not long ago, and I understand that Maurice Chevalier will play it at the *Comédie Française* in Paris.

Some of our most popular comedians have typed themselves as "stock" characters; they improvise within their adopted roles. Past masters in this field are Jack Benny, Bob Hope, Eddie Cantor. Famous clowns who have exploited their special physical characteristics are "Schnozzle" Durante, Joe E. Brown, Martha Raye, Bert

Lahr. Their professional ancestry dates back centuries but their humor is as modern as tomorrow's news.

The ultimate in ladylike clowning can be enjoyed in the impeccable artistry of Beatrice Lillie. Clowns are born, not made. Her humor is creative; seldom has a woman been blessed with so unique a gift.

Imogene Coca and Sid Caesar are in a class by themselves. They too have the creative gift. Caesar's ability to rearrange what is essentially hackneyed material, making of it something that is irresistibly funny, is in the best *Commedia dell' arte* tradition.

An undertone of melancholy frequently runs through the personalities of these comedians who might be imagined in a state of perpetual and hilarious mirth. The only time I ever met Maurice Chevalier in private life my impression was of a very quiet, serious-minded man, which makes his urbane gaiety on the stage and screen even more interesting. Moreover, in seeing his one-man show at the Town Hall in New York, several of his little vignettes revealed what a really fine actor he is. Danny Kaye, too, has his thoughtful side, according to report. It is a serious business, it seems, this being a comic.

You have no doubt heard the story of the most famous of all clowns, Debureau, but it bears repeating here.

A noted neurologist in Paris was visited by a sad-looking man who complained of persistent insomnia and overwhelming melancholia. The doctor, after considerable questioning, told him: "You are not ill, my friend—you simply need gaiety, cheering up! You need to laugh. Go see the famous Debureau tonight." To which his patient replied: "I cannot, *Monsieur le docteur*. You see, I am Debureau."

Comedy can become a very thoughtful weapon. Take the *Lysistrata* of Aristophanes, written and produced in 400 B.C.

The women of Greece have become fed up with the lonely lives they have been forced to lead during the twenty years' war between Athens and Sparta. They determine to do something about their situation.

Lysistrata has learned that a temporary truce is about to be declared; husbands and lovers will return for a brief respite from war. Inspired by Lysistrata, the women of the various cities barricade themselves in the temple of Athena, refusing to have anything to do with their returning husbands and lovers until a binding treaty of peace has been signed. The women win.

They end the war.

It is hard to realize that *Lysistrata* was first performed more than two thousand years ago. If the Athenians had stopped laughing long enough to learn the lesson of the play, they might have changed history. We might now be living in a world governed by the serene beauty and the lofty philosophic concepts of those ancient Greeks.

Although basic comedy remains eternally fresh, its dialogue is often perishable. Idioms and colloquialisms change over the years; some types of jokes and verbal colloquialisms go out of style. A risqué story of a hundred years ago may be meaningless today. Some of Shakespeare's rowdy jokes which, if understood, might upset his most ardent admirers, are so out of date that we miss their significance and pass them by.

A great director-playwright once said to me, "Almost anyone can play tragedy if it is great enough. But comedy?

It is a science like mathematics. You add two to two and it must make four. You must be born with the instinct that tells you what timing to use. You must know what to seem to throw away in order to get your laughs."

Often a player will go to his director when the play has been running for awhile and say, "I'm not getting the laugh I used to get on that line. What am I doing that's making me lose it?" (Or it may be some piece of business which is missing fire.) The director watches a performance to see what the actor or some fellow performer is doing or not doing which interferes with the audience reaction. He may call a brief rehearsal for the actors involved in the matter in question. A short discussion may be sufficient to clear up the difficulty or it may be necessary to go through the troublesome scene in order to recapture the original timing or mood. This is a fairly common occurrence. For once an audience has honestly laughed at a given place in the play, we, back of the footlights, know that the laugh is there. Our job is to keep it there, every performance.

But laugh reactions of an audience are unpredictable. George M. Cohan, the famous "Yankee Doodle Dandy," who enlivened the theatre of the twenties, was a master of farce techniques. Yet he once produced a serious play called *The Tavern,* with unforeseeable results. On the opening night, somewhere in the course of the first act, the audience began to titter; then it went into gales of laughter. Mr. Cohan, who was not appearing in the play, rushed backstage during the first intermission. The order went out: "Play the whole thing for laughs." The actors were evidently clever enough to perform this mental somersault, for *The Tavern* had a successful run.

Essentially, a man's sense of humor is pretty much

47

the same in any place or period, and good comedy will win your laughter no matter where you were born or what language you speak. But good comedies are rare; some seem heavy-handed, obvious, or shop-worn. The lack may be in the writing, the direction, or the actors' inadequacies. You leave the theatre, vaguely dissatisfied, yet you may not know why.

It looks so easy, so spontaneous. One cannot expect an audience to realize how hard it is to create comedy in the first place, and to project it in the second. In fact, it is part of an actor's business not to let you realize it. Comedy requires great discipline, delicate timing. It is the most difficult of any type of theatre expression.

When it's good, comedy goes beyond mere laughter. Except for the most elementary kinds—the custard-pie school to which I've referred—you can and should get more than amusement from a comedy, something which stays with you. You may see a little of yourself in the play; your appreciation of life and of people around you may have deepened.

Puck, in *A Midsummer Night's Dream,* says, "What fools these mortals be!" And he laughs.

Well, let's face it. We are fools. We behave foolishly—all of us. And we need to be able to laugh, lovingly, understandingly, at ourselves and at each other.

The Making of Magic

T HERE IS ONE magical moment in the world of make-believe which never fails to thrill me. I am sitting with you in the audience. The lights go down. The buzz of conversation dies away. This is the moment of expectancy. Wonderful things may happen. A new star may appear in the theatrical skies tonight, a great new playwright may be discovered. The curtain rises and the play begins.

But how many of you in the audience have any idea of the intricate steps that have led up to this magic moment? Let me see if I can trace them for you.

Obviously, the author's play is the primary base on

which rests all that follows. But nowadays the mechanics of getting a play on are so complicated, so full of pitfalls and unpredictable contingencies, that the poor author must feel at times he has been consigned to limbo. Usually, he is on hand to make cuts and changes, the need for which may develop as the rehearsals progress. Some authors are helpful and cooperative, ready to follow suggestions from the director, sometimes even from members of the cast—suggestions which may enhance the value of what he has written. But occasionally—and this is usually in proportion to his inexperience—he clings so tenaciously to his beautiful words that he becomes a problem child to both director and players.

An experienced author is much more likely to disappear into the back rows of the orchestra, get busy with his fountain pen, and come back to rehearsal with what may turn out to be one of his best scenes. This is professionalism.

On the other hand, I recall one author whose first play (I might add the only one he has ever had produced) needed drastic revision after the out-of-town try-out where all the shortcomings of the play had revealed themselves. Just prior to the New York opening a conference took place between the author, the manager, and the director. Eight grueling hours were spent in analyzing what was wrong with the script. At the end of the session the author finally agreed to make the essential changes. Rehearsals were suspended for two days in order to give him time to do this. After those two days he turned up with two typewritten pages containing superficial alterations which solved nothing. The play suffered seriously as a result. It ran a few brief weeks, at the end of which a closing notice was posted and fifty-two actors were out of work.

But the author always has the final word as to what changes can be made in his play; his Dramatist Guild contract sees to that.

The more experienced an author is the more ready he is to make changes, once he is convinced that the changes are needed. He has learned that "plays are not written, they are rewritten."

But in spite of all hazards, producers do go on producing plays.

It happens more or less in this fashion. After reading countless manuscripts, a producer decides that a particular play must be done. Arthur Hopkins, one of the most distinguished of theatre men, used to say that this was the *only* reason for producing a play. Having fallen in love with a manuscript, the producer's problems really begin.

First there is the task of finding backers. Nowadays very few producers invest their own money—at any rate not all the money the budgeting calls for. The cost of producing plays has risen so astronomically that the financial risk is shared by several small investors. He may first try to engage some well-known star as a lure to backers who are looking for a "sure thing." Some of the investors are theatre people who may themselves have had a finger in the producing game and consider themselves to be fairly good judges of what makes for a box-office script. These people may invest several thousand dollars. Smaller "outsiders"—obscure friends of the management, possibly the secretary to the producer, or his barber or his dentist, may gamble only a few hundred. Investing in a play is always a gamble. No one's judgment is infallible.

There is a story in circulation among theatre people that during the out-of-town try-out of *Oklahoma!,* the fabulous musical which Rodgers and Hammerstein made out of Lynn Riggs's play, *Green Grow the Lilacs,* you could have had a "piece" of it for five hundred dollars. It ran for about five years on Broadway and toured all over the country. A smash hit of this sort repays its investors a thousand-fold.

A play like John van Druten's *Voice of the Turtle* is a veritable gold mine for all concerned: a one-set play requiring only three actors. Four or five road companies drew audiences for several years and the play is still popular on the "straw hat" circuits.

Once the money has been raised, the producer's responsibilities increase. He must assemble, within the agreed-upon budget, the director he believes in, the best actors he can beg, borrow, cajole, or just plain cast. In some instances, he relies on a movie name or two to insure in advance the public's interest.

This has proven to be a fallacious theory over and over again. Even accomplished actors and actresses who enjoy film reputations have proved to be "no draw" when the vehicle in which they appeared failed to please the critics. The return of Fredric March to the legitimate stage after many years of success in the movies is an example. His name and the vehicle in which he appeared had been widely publicized in advance, but the notices for the play itself were unanimously bad. So bad that Freddie, with engaging candor, bought a large space in one of the foremost New York dailies to reproduce a cartoon borrowed from *The New Yorker*. It showed two trapeze artists, one at the top corner of the space, one far below. The latter had failed to come into contact with his fellow-aerialist, swinging at the top of the column, who smiled apologetically at his partner as the latter was crashing to his doom, and murmured the brief caption, *"Oops! Sorry!"* Never have I known a star to accept failure so gracefully and so amusingly.

But to get back to our play. There are compromises in the course of the casting period. The ideal cast seldom materializes. Its cost might be prohibitive, making any eventual profit to the investors impossible. However, it is a good idea to read a play with a "dream cast" in one's imagination; that costs nothing as yet and makes the manuscript come to life more vividly. I myself have collaborated on a dramatization of one of Balzac's novels. My ideal cast would include Charles Laughton, Ingrid Bergman, Maurice Chevalier, Judith Anderson, and Brigitte Bardot, or, preferably, Vivian Leigh. You can imagine what such a cast would cost! These are the players whom I visualize whenever I reread the play. In the process they and the play seem very good indeed. You might try doing this someday, with any play you like.

Let us assume that a fine, or at least an adequate, cast has been assembled, one which represents the fewest possible compromises; that all the arguments about salaries and billing have finally been settled. Naturally, the director has been in consultation with the producer for some time. Some producers are also directors—Joshua Logan, for instance.

Any successful producer has listings of players whose work has interested him in the past. On the other hand, he may be willing to take a chance on an "unknown" who seems to be exactly the right type when he or she first walks into his office.

David Belasco was famous for his "discoveries" as well as for the over-all high quality of his casts. I once questioned a famous character actor about this. He had been with Belasco for years. The actor gave me a sly wink. "What's the Guv'nor's secret?" He was echoing my own question. "He just engages four-hundred-dollar-a-week actors for forty-dollar parts. That way you can't go wrong." I couldn't help feeling that there was a little more to it than that.

Once the news that a new play is about to be produced goes out over the grapevine, the producer's office is likely to be besieged by anxious and eager thespians. Some producers, however, work through only one particular casting agent, seeing no one who has not been sent by his agency. Nevertheless, endless numbers of "unrepresented" actors continue to flood his office, always hoping, with the eternal optimism of their profession, that the producer may change his mind and give them a chance to read for him.

The favored player for whom the agent has made an appointment weaves his way at the appointed hour through the crowded waiting room outside the great man's inner sanctum. Under a barrage of envious eyes the lucky one slips through the door to which he alone has the magic word, "Appointment."

Once the cast has been chosen rehearsals begin. Much depends upon the man in charge. The ideal director should be a person blessed with tact, with immense patience, and with a thorough knowledge of the techniques of acting. He might be likened to a fine orchestra leader who knows precisely how the various instruments should be played. I need not tell you how rare a phenomenon such a director is. The late Max Reinhardt, the great German producer-director of *The Miracle* and *Everyman*, was such a one, I believe. Within the limits of his taste David Belasco was another. Today Elia Kazan and Joshua Logan are outstanding. All of these men have known how to get the best out of their actors.

In this sprawling, time-consuming rehearsal period, it is the director who must bring order out of seeming chaos. He must have a clear concept of what he wants and an over-all plan for achieving it. He must understand the structure of the play as it is written and then he must make action and words contribute to that structure.

The cast is now assembled. Some of the players know each other, others meet for the first time. But everyone is nervous. There is that worrisome trial period of five days during which the producer is allowed by the Actors' Equity Association to replace any player without giving a reason or paying any salary. This is a terrifying time during which no actor is at his best. But it is a necessary interval, one that is designed to protect the producer against a possible mistake in judgment. It is an optional privilege, not always used. One sensitive, understanding producer-director started his rehearsals with this brief and reassuring speech: "Boys and girls, I want you all to relax. There will be no changes in the cast. Each of you has been carefully selected because you are the best possible choice for the part. You are set as from today. Now let's get down to business." You can imagine how that cast was willing to work!

At the first reading, sides, the typewritten parts used by each player, are handed out. The play is read through by the entire cast. Presently chairs are placed in positions which indicate the setting in which the action of the scene will occur. The actors fumble their way through the script. Now they tackle the first act. From then on, rehearsals proceed steadily. When the positions of the players are tentatively "set"—and this may take as long as a week—the director begins to get an idea of what the rhythm, the mood, the movement of the play will be.

The rules of the Actors' Equity Association permit four weeks of rehearsal; after that, with rare exceptions, full salaries must be paid. This is a period of intense activity. Four weeks is a short time in which to build a house of the imagination—one that must sometimes give the impression of having been lived in for decades. The great Russian director, Constantin Stanislavsky, once said, when he heard how we in America are assembled as a new company for each play, "How can you do it in four weeks? In my theatre we can take four to six months to prepare a play. It would not be surprising if you had few great performances. The miracle would be that you had any."

Different directors use different methods in manipulating their material. One will come to rehearsal with a clear blue-print of what he wants; every movement, almost every inflection, has been worked out in his mind beforehand. The task of his actors is to carry out his plans. Another type of director quietly waits to see what the actor himself will bring to the play as he becomes familiar with it. The true artist may travel a long way from that first fumbling reading, since much depends on what he gets from his fellow players. His own responses are conditioned by what goes on around him.

For better or worse, this is the only way I personally can work. Once and only once did I accept from the very beginning the pattern of performance laid out for me by a well-meaning director in whom I had faith. After four weeks of conscientious effort on both our parts, I gave a very bad, constricted performance, although I had tried very hard indeed to carry out his design for the part. Someone else might have done it successfully. I couldn't.

Once I rehearsed with a director, quite a young one, who had obviously imbibed many theories of the Russian school—theories which must be very helpful when one has four or five months in which to prepare a play. After the first reading he sent us home with instructions to work out and bring back in writing analyses of the lives and behavior patterns of the characters we were playing, prior to our opening scenes, and after our final ones—assuming that the character had not died in the course of the play.

Some of his cast declined to bring in the "home work" he requested. Oddly enough, their performances proved to be the most effective of all. Good actors do this kind of work subconsciously, in the privacy of their imaginations; they do not need to put anything on paper, or even into words.

Each gifted person has something special to contribute. Think of the many Hamlets who have brilliantly played that part. I have seen fourteen Hamlets, not all of them equally good but each showing some facet of that complex character which justified his attempting it. Incidentally, no one has ever been hopelessly bad as Hamlet. Shakespeare saw to that!

But even a clever director can sometimes overlook values which are hidden in a script. One of the most sensitive and helpful men I ever worked with was Dudley Digges. A fine actor himself, he led you gently into the heart of the play and then left you to your own devices. In that first memorable production of *The Wild Duck* in 1925, he spent hours on the scene toward the end of the second act, the scene where Gregers Werle interrogates his old friend, Hjalmar Ekdahl, about Hjalmar's marriage to Gina, the former servant in Gregers' home. This is a scene with subtle undercurrents. The two men, seated across the table from each other, pay little attention to Gina, the wife (the part I was playing). She sits above them, quietly mending socks.

At the dress rehearsal, Mr. Digges came to me and said amusedly, "Here I've been thinking all along that it is the dialogue between those two men which is important. Sitting out front, I've realized that the chief thing holding my attention is the effect of what they are saying on your face." I was as surprised as he. And of course gratified.

By the third week of rehearsal all the players have pretty well "jelled" their conceptions of the parts. The perfecting of these concepts goes on indefinitely; even after the play has opened a performance may increase in stature or deepen in emotional content. If it is a comedy the laughs become sure-fire. If one is doing an emotional role the feeling grows stronger, its effect more moving. To the professional the four grinding weeks of work—the hours spent in darkened, empty theatres—are supplemented by almost as many hours of study on the outside. There is no nine-to-five routine for any one involved. In fact, there are times when you could use a good thirty-six-hour day!

As the weeks run their course, work grows more intensive. During the last week before the opening, rehearsals may run into the wee small hours. By three A.M. coffee has been consumed in endless quantities. The stained and crumpled cardboard coffee containers litter the backstage area. Only a few bleak work lights are on. The director's tired voice calls through the darkness, "Do it again . . . No, let's try it this way . . . No, that's not quite it. Let's take it again."

The faces of the cast are drawn with fatigue. The women look white and haggard. There are circles under everyone's eyes.

To the uninitiated all this may seem glamorous and perhaps even a little mad. People who, three and a half weeks ago, may have met as complete strangers have now been drawn into the intimacy of daily, unremittting work. In the process of doing a play together actors and other collaborators see far more of each other than they would in months, even years, of ordinary social contacts. They see at close quarters each others' weaknesses as well as strengths. Patience may, under great pressure, be taxed beyond the call of duty, yet I have seen courtesy and a quiet voice prevail in the face of great provocation. On the other hand, there are few of us in the theatre who have not encountered selfishness and ruthlessness. Surprisingly enough, they sometimes rear their ugly heads in very high places.

While the cast and the director are going through their paces, a whole staff of unseen workers are equally busy. The costume designer has conferred with the head of the chosen costume house. Some costumes are taken from stock, others are made to order. Time is set aside for fittings. It is a hectic period for both stellar and bit players.

The publicity man has been placing stories in newspapers and magazines. The business manager has for weeks been preparing a list of carefully chosen names for the distribution of opening night tickets. A large block of choice seats is always reserved for the "gentlemen of the press," the theatre critics, each of whom receives two complimentary tickets which permit him to bring his wife or a friend. Among the "civilian" public, certain "famous first-nighters" are allowed to purchase seats in favored locations. Members of the cast are permitted to buy a very limited number of seats for opening night. (Family and friends are prone to assume that actors get these tickets "for free." They couldn't be more mistaken.)

On the night of dress rehearsal excitement runs high. Everyone shares in it. The stagehands and electricians now take over. All the mechanical details must run smoothly, handled by men trained in the use of lighting effects, of offstage sound machines. The work of each is important; a mistake by any one of them may ruin a scene.

This all-important dress rehearsal, which is the final

summing up of weeks of work, is usually called on the night before the opening performance. It is the director's chance to time the performance of the play and to iron out any last-minute problems. It is in this rehearsal that new values reveal themselves. Sometimes, for a short space, the performance which has been so carefully built up during all these weeks seems to fall to pieces. There are fresh problems—moving about on the actual set, handling unfamiliar props, climbing up and down stairways which may prove to be too narrow or too frail. All these new complications seem to destroy the smoothly flowing rhythms so painstakingly achieved during those four weeks' work. If one is lucky enough to have an out-of-town try-out of a week or more, these difficulties can be resolved, and the play can recapture the flow of those last pre-dress rehearsal days. More than one play, however, is denied this "practice period," and usually pays dearly for the forced economy of which it is the victim. I have seen opening night performances which proved disastrous; two weeks later, if the play was still on, one might be charmed by it.

A specific example of this was Constance Collier's dramatization of George Du Maurier's famous novel, *Peter Ibbetson*. In it there were dream sequences in which Peter and the Duchess were shown as children in an occasional flashback. Those scenes were played behind a gauze scrim. Both John Barrymore and Constance Collier, in the leading roles, had a popular following and the first-night audience was unusually distinguished. On opening night the scrim curtains got all fouled up—movable platforms refused to budge; finally the whole "dream" mechanism collapsed, the curtain was lowered, and the stage manager came out to make a speech of apology.

Next night all had been straightened out and one of John Barrymore's most touching performances became the talk of the town.

At the dress rehearsal the director and the head designer are watching the performance from the front. They take careful notes, and after the final curtain has fallen the cast assembles to hear them, to correct mistakes, to polish a scene. This is an ordeal, but much is accomplished at this session, even though it sometimes lasts all night.

Finally the performers are dismissed to get some much-needed rest; and of course they must be given time to attend to essential chores of grooming. Light changes are reviewed with the crew. The very air is charged with excitement.

Opening night is now upon us. Backstage, telegrams are delivered in a steady stream; boxes of flowers pile up in the corners of dressing rooms. It is eight-thirty and the stage manager calls, "Places, please." A last pat of powder, a final exchange of good wishes. Out front the house lights are lowered. An expectant silence prevails. The curtains part and the play begins.

The next two hours and a half will be decisive. For some they may mean a bare living, for others affluence and increased reputations. For there are no "nice little successes" in the theatre any more. One is either in a hit or a flop. If a play receives "mixed notices," it may struggle along for two or three weeks in the hope that some portion of the public to which it might appeal will find its way to the theatre in sufficient numbers to at least pay the running expenses. But only a few productions survive this treatment; few are successful in weathering a slow start. Managers have grown poorer and wiser after a few such valiant attempts to woo reluctant ticket-buyers.

But what can equal the wave of encouragement which pours into one's life when the morning papers contain unanimous "raves"? One knows that a line is forming at the box office; the telephone rings incessantly. One would think the heavens themselves had brightened. And indeed they may have done just that! For it is in successful plays that a new star is born and that older ones go on to increased fame and fortune.

From that point on, it will be the newly recognized star's greatest problem to pick only successful plays in which to appear. You would be amazed to know how many careers have foundered on that very rock! Stars must develop a kind of sixth sense about the box-office value of plays if they are to continue their climb to a secure place in the affections of the public. One success does not do it, and selection is not easy. The actor is prone to fall in love with a part rather than a play. This is dangerous. A few failures and the brightness of his overnight success has dimmed. He may have to do it all over again.

I once asked an experienced playwright why it is so hard to find a good play. His answer was succinct, albeit profane.

"Because they're damned hard to write!"

Movie Magic

T HE THEATRE MARQUEE is ablaze with light. Long, sleek motorcars come to a slow stop at the curb. Incredibly beautiful women in sumptuous furs emerge, escorted by men in evening clothes. Policemen make a passage for them through crowds straining to spot favorite movie stars, who pause for a moment to be identified and interviewed before a battery of microphones and newsreel cameras. Squeals and cries of "There she is! Look, there he comes!" punctuate the hubbub. I hardly need identify this scene as a typical movie premiere—a fairly routine performance ever since Hollywood glamour first hit the headlines.

Behind this synthetic glitter stands a whole army of people, known and unknown, who work from dawn to dusk, five days a week, to bring you the picture you saw last night at your neighborhood movie theatre.

How did you like the movie? What did you get from it? Were you moved by the story? Or by an actor's performance? Did you care what happened to the characters you were watching—and if not, why not? Was your interest sustained? Did you carry away any memorable impressions? Did the picture enlarge your understanding of human nature and of the problems of humanity in general? Or did you merely sit in a comfortable loge seat to while away an evening?

Movies have come a long, long way since the days of the first Hollywood premiere. Today you have a greater variety of subjects and treatments to choose from than ever before. Slapstick comedies and horror films will probably always be made for a public which is willing to pay to see them. But for the discriminating there is a wide range of adult entertainment from which to make your choice. The movies have come of age.

No longer are we likely to be shown fabricated imitations of foreign backgrounds built on the movie lot. We actually see Africa in *The Nun's Story,* Japan in *Sayonara,* Norway in *The Vikings.* Authentic backgrounds bring the whole world into our own neighborhoods. Foreign films give us an enlarged understanding of the way other people live and think. And Shakespeare, through the films, has been brought into the experience of thousands of people who would never think of reading *Henry V, Hamlet,* or *Julius Caesar.*

Foreign players of the calibre of Pierre Fresnay, Jean Gabin, and Anna Magnani bring us fresh revelations of acting techniques. Pictures like *Open City* and *The Bicycle Thief* drive home to us the pathos of underprivileged humanity, evoking a sympathy for the little fellow which we may not have felt before. Pictures like *Grand Illusion,* with its universal theme of war and its futility, puncture the drum-beating concept of war's nobility which has so long dominated the thinking of man.

Great themes are also dramatized in mature American films. *On the Waterfront,* which further emphasized Marlon Brando's acting talents, exposes corruption in the field of organized labor. *Sayonara* and *The Defiant Ones* show up the evils of racial prejudice. In a more romantic treatment, the movie version of *South Pacific* does the same thing. *Twelve Angry Men* is a striking plea for a sense of responsibility toward a fellow creature regardless of social status. And in the film version of *The Old Man and The Sea,* Spencer Tracy's superlative honesty measures itself against Ernest Hemingway's lofty theme, the indestructibility of the human spirit.

The change in style which has taken place in screen acting during the last thirty years or so was brought home to me when I attended a reshowing of Oscar Wilde's *Salomé.* In this silent picture, made in 1923, a great actress, Alla Nazimova, produced and starred in a film which was a daring departure from the popular fare of that day. Great as her talent indubitably was, to my modern eye she seemed synthetically "sexy," and more affected than effective. The performances of her fellow players, excellent actors all, seemed exaggerated to the point of "hamminess." We have grown accustomed to a much more restrained style of acting. Today's vastly improved lighting and camera techniques bring us a variety of effects, modulating those effects with much more subtlety.

In order to get the most out of this expanding cinema world which the screen with all its miracles of technical progress brings you today, you in your turn should develop an increasing capacity for appreciation. Appreciation requires a mind open to things unfamiliar. A vastly wider range of enjoyment is possible to you if you exercise selectivity in your choice of the films you support. Good taste grows through what it feeds upon and becomes increasingly exacting.

As a movie viewer, not only am I conscious of the immediate action before my eyes; I know that there is a vast and complicated machinery behind the mysterious screen I am watching. The many steps required in the making of a movie may be a surprise to the uninitiated, as they were to me when I first went to Hollywood. Whenever a scene builds steadily toward a big emotional climax, it becomes the more remarkable to me because of my knowledge of how it was done. Parts of the scene were undoubtedly taken on different days, others having been shot in between. Seldom has the achieved climax been made in unbroken sequence. The taking of long-shots and close-ups frequently interrupts the flow of a scene. Sometimes an expensive set, in which different scenes take place, must be utilized while it is still standing. All these are important factors to be considered by a producer, who is trying to stay within his budget.

The basic appeal of a motion picture is and must be

visual. "Never say it if you can show it" is a precept in the industry. Producers know that movie audiences primarily want to look, not listen.

The first step in the making of a film must necessarily be the selection of a story, although a mere idea for a story may strike the producer as interesting enough for him to buy. In any event, he secures the rights to the material and sets to work. He calls in a scenarist whose speciality it is to whip the idea or story into a screen treatment.

During the many story conferences which follow, the script is "kicked around" and examined from every angle by a small group of people who have been in on the story from the beginning.

"Is it box office?"

"Can we get Spencer?"

"Nope, he's tied up."

"Then who is available?"

"What about Bob, or Greg, or Jimmie?"

And so it goes—on and on and on—while the scenarist quietly goes mad.

Presently the whole proposition is submitted to the "money people." These may be either the heads of a big studio with which a producer is affiliated, or they may represent bankers who, I am told, are frequently behind the financing of a motion picture. The financiers agree to put up X number of dollars for the budget. This budget may be as little as $50,000 for a "quickie," or $3,000,000 for a major production. Finally these matters are settled and the producer can say, "We're in business."

Sometimes the director and the writer are one man.

In any case, producer and director negotiate with stars and leading players whom they consider most suitable for the parts called for by the story. Central Casting, the actors' registry bureau in Hollywood, is notified of the number and types of extras needed. Bit parts may be cast by the assistant director, although the director himself usually gives those selected the final once-over.

The mechanical crew is now organized. The head cameraman is of paramount importance; some stars even stipulate in their contracts which one they prefer, having had happy results with him on previous pictures. If there are important out-of-door scenes the best possible location is found, to which in due time everyone involved is transported. A second crew, consisting of "stand-ins," who take the place of the principal actors when lights are being arranged, stunt people—experts in doing difficult physical feats which might endanger the neck or limbs of some valuable star—all these auxiliary folk go on location along with the regular members of the organization. In the background are script girls, make-up artists, hairdressers, grips, sometimes even mothers of the children who are in the cast. If there are child actors involved, the Board of Education requires that a teacher go along to make sure that the youngsters do not fall behind in their school work.

Weeks, even months, may be consumed in takes and re-takes. Unforeseeable delays may occur. Some one may be taken ill or hurt in an accident; the weather refuses to cooperate—in outdoor scenes a cloudy day is a catastrophe. When *Song of Bernadette,* in which I appeared with Jennifer Jones, was being done on the 20th-Century Fox lot, it was brought home to me how modern inventions can create a problem which adds considerably to the cost of a film. All the grotto scenes in this picture were taken out in the open, on the back of the lot. Several hundred people—extras playing villagers, as well as principals—were scattered over the scene. All of us would be standing ready, waiting for the cameras to start rolling. Suddenly the sound man's voice would be heard. "Hold everything! Plane coming."

Not a sound could we hear. Only the delicate mechanism of the sound man's equipment could detect the distant droning of the approaching plane. All of us, actors and crew, had to stand waiting for the plane to appear and disappear, waiting until the sound had faded out beyond the reach of even the sound man's keen ear. Then and only then could we proceed with the scene. Delays such as this occur many times in the course of shooting a picture. They add thousands of dollars to the expense of a film.

Finally (and in these days of economy drives this comes sooner than it used to), all the scenes numbered in the working script are on celluloid, and the word goes out, "Fold 'em. We're through."

But the producer, the director, the head cameraman, are far from through. The cutter and the film editor enter upon the scene. They are very important figures in preparing a picture for the market.

Now begins the trying period of matching together the best pieces of celluloid; every inch of "take" has to be examined and its value to the total effect judged. The director and the cutter usually sit in on this together.

A composer writes the incidental music, the musical background for the film, then scores it. Process shots (brief scenes taken in close-up against a painted scene drop) may have to be added. Additional dialogue may be dubbed in.

I myself had a horrifying experience when I played the Mexican mother in *The Furies* with Barbara Stanwyck and Walter Huston. My instructions had been to speak my lines in straight, unaccented English. Imagine the shock, some ten days after the picture was finished, when I was called back to re-do all my speeches—"cold," standing alone in a darkened sound studio, in my street clothes, carefully watching my mouth movements on the screen so as to be able to duplicate my own performance, but this time using a pronounced Mexican accent. And all the scenes were powerful emotional ones, not easy to do under any circumstances. But under these—! Which just goes to show that you can do anything if you have to.

During the putting together of a picture, the sound track is constantly being checked in order to make sure that the volume is exactly right and to take care of any overlapping of dialogue which may have crept in. It may take a year, sometimes even longer, to bring a picture from its inception as an idea to its final state. By this time all the players and the crew have dispersed to other jobs, or merely to enjoy the "resting" period which is the distasteful alternative to activity.

After a few "sneak" previews in some more or less remote movie houses to test out the reactions of audiences, a gala opening may be arranged. These premieres vary in lavishness and showmanship in proportion to the importance of the stars or of the producer.

There is one thing about movie-making of which you, as a part of the audience, are seldom aware. To become cognizant of such fine points is part of your critical development.

On the screen an actor can seldom give a great performance without the influence of a fine director. A knowledgeable movie director selects his players so wisely, manipulates their performances so cleverly, that you, watching the result, may accept as an acting achievement something which is simply a good piece of tailor-made type casting.

Recently I had occasion to see for the second time a picture which had received accolades on several counts. "Oscars" had been showered upon nearly every one connected with it. I had carried away an impression of a tense story dominated by a performance of quiet power. Seeing the film again with more analytical eyes and ears, and with less absorption in the story itself, I felt a little like the child in the Andersen fairy tale who, as the Emperor rides by in what every one has been told is a fabulous new costume, cries out, "But the King has no clothes on!"

The story of the film still held me; the music added immeasurably to the tension which the director had created. But I became conscious of the fact that the acting of the leading role wasn't acting, in the accepted sense of the word. A taciturn man, perfectly cast as to physical type, was called upon to walk through scene after scene, pathetically alone. Through empty streets he wanders, isolated from his fellow villagers. Never was a picture more right visually. The director had selected his player so wisely, the scenario was so tightly written, the music so heightened the intensity of the situation, that only after a detached re-evaluation did I realize that what seemed to be a brilliant piece of acting was primarily a brilliant piece of type-casting. (Once again I was conscious of the fact that in the movies the appeal is essentially visual.)

This is not to say that there is not wisdom in such type-casting. A good actor of course has his own concept of the part, but it is the director who has the final say. In the end, it is the director's concept which prevails.

Once a screen performance is seen by the public, a film actor cannot alter or modify it. This is not true of the stage actor. For all the trials and difficulties before an opening night, a stage performance is susceptible to modification in ensuing performances. Sooner or later, the stage actor is on his own. Once that curtain is up he must "deliver" in every scene in which he is involved—until the curtain comes down again. A director may have helped him to exceed his own average capabilities, may have given him invaluable guidance. But the almost physical relationship brought about by immediate contact with a live audience inspires a kind of creative acting which can rise, through repetition, to increasing heights.

But in the movies it is different. When the actors come to the set they run through their lines briefly, then go through the scene a few times for the director. Presently he says, "Okay, let's shoot it." Some of the actors have arrived on the set without even having memorized their lines. In fact, some of the most experienced do this deliberately; they feel that too much rehearsing of a scene results in a lack of spontaneity, that they may grow stale.

After a few brief run-throughs, the director calls out, "Camera! Action!" The scene begins. Someone fluffs his lines. "Cut!" the director calls. It begins all over again. "Camera! Action!" A small, built-in audience is always there—director, crew, onlookers, rim the set. Sometimes as many as five or six cameras are focused on a scene in order to get it from different angles. After several efforts the director finally says, "Print that one"—welcome words which tell you he is satisfied.

But the performance, as the public sees it, is as good as the cutter of the film has permitted it to be, as good as what he leaves in the film. It is a disheartening experience to learn that what the actor feels to be the best parts of his characterization are lying on the cutting-room floor.

I remember doing a film in which a most telling and artistically effective scene had been made. I had been thrilled with it during its filming. It had a dramatic beginning, a logical build-up, and a quiet, powerful finish. When I saw the uncut film run off, I said to the director, "Do anything you want to me, leave my name off the credits—*anything*—but promise me you won't cut down that scene."

The picture was a melodramatic one, based on the activities of the infamous Barker-Karpis gang, whose story is told in J. Edgar Hoover's case histories of crime in America. Evidently the quiet key in which the scene I speak of was played did not appeal to the cutter. After all, wasn't this a cops-and-robbers picture? When the film was shown, two-thirds of the sequence reposed in the cutting-room wastebasket, and my chances of becoming a female Edward G. Robinson had evaporated.

Yes, the cutter is a very important member of the staff. In some cases, even directors must defer to him.

From the actor's viewpoint at least, a screen performance is an edited performance. Upon the director, the cutter, the film editors, depend the final shape and quality of the entire movie. Their decisions determine the final effectiveness of the individual actors.

A major problem for the movie director is the duplication of reality, and his resources for creating it are very great indeed. If a scene showing the Alps is needed, the Alps can be had. If a forest fire is called for, the technicians light one. Everything is controlled by experts. The magnificent reality we see today on the screen is the result of a gradual expansion of technical knowledge and a fantastic expenditure of money for experimenting. With the steady development of color processes and the marvels of stereophonic sound, the screen is showing us horizons never dreamed of by the pioneers in this field.

In the early days of movie making, things were done much more simply. Outdoor scenes were photographed in their natural settings, which of course is the reason why the industry grew up in California. Assured of almost continual sunshine, a director could round up a few actors and one or two actresses (or just some photogenic girls), find a good location spot, cook up a story, sometimes "off the cuff" as he went along—and lo, there was a picture!

The progress that has been made since those early days is a miracle. Settings create almost unbelievable illusions. When I was doing *Song of Bernadette* I used to feel, when I arrived on the lot at seven in the morning, that I was strolling into a little French village. Seven or eight streets led down to the central square. In one was the church, beyond it the mill, and beyond that a little lake where ducks were paddling and women were washing clothes on the rocks. I had the feeling that I was spending the summer in France, in a village where, through some curious circumstance, every one spoke English.

I felt the same way during the filming of David O. Selznick's production of *A Tale of Two Cities*. Streets leading to the Bastille prison were lined with houses two or three stories high. The citizens of Paris leaned out of the windows to watch the rioting mobs. The authenticity was impressive. Here was a triumph of realistic staging.

Speaking of *A Tale of Two Cities,* never was a babe in the woods more uninformed about the terrain she was entering than was I when Mr. Selznick engaged me to play Madame De Farge, that unhappy woman who has come to be the symbol of the French Revolution's unleashed terror.

A friend of mine was playing an engagement with Alla Nazimova. One day Nazimova said to him, "I have been offered the part of Madame De Farge in *A Tale of Two Cities.* I am not right for it. It must be somebody physically larger, stronger, than I could ever seem to be. Why don't you tell your friend Blanche Yurka to contact the Selznick office?" He did. So did I. Result: a test for the part was arranged for me in a small studio on West Fifty-sixth Street in New York, one frequently used by big picture companies for just this purpose.

I was completely green at the movie game. I did not know until months later that sixty-seven other actresses had already been tested for the part. But I was excited; any new challenge always stimulates my imagination.

So I "boned up" on the Dickens novel, visualizing the experiences through which that bitter, vengeful woman must have passed to have become what she was at the time we meet her in the story. One day I went to the testing studio to consult with the make-up man as to how we could best transform my rather dignified blonde appearance into what I conceived Madame De Farge to look like.

Two scenes were used for the screen test. The first took place in the wineshop of the De Farges where

Madame De Farge warily answers questions put to her by a stranger. In her cap is a small rose, the signal agreed upon by the *Jacquerie* as a warning of danger.

It was a quiet, controlled scene, shot through with undercurrents of menace. My costume was to be a drab woolen dress with a simple fichu of the period, and a cotton mobcap to keep my smooth black hair tidy.

The second part of the test was the Tribunal scene. In it Madame De Farge, realizing that the scion of the Evremonde family is about to be given his freedom, leaps onto the judges' stand to utter her bitter denunciation of this, the last living member of the family of aristocrats which had liquidated every one of her kin. She produces the evidence against "the Evremonde" and demands that Charles Evremonde, the last of the line, be sentenced to the *guillotine.*

Passing along the corridor to the make-up room, I heard a familiar voice speaking Madame's lines to the judges. Surreptiously, I peeked through the curtains to see who it was. A very famous tragedienne was in the midst of her test for the Tribunal scene. I noted that she was still wearing the tidy cap and dress of the wineshop sequence. Instantly I knew what I wanted to do.

I slipped away to see the make-up man and to inspect the black wig I was to wear. I then spoke to the person in charge of wardrobe. I asked that the fichu for my costume be made of a cheap, flimsy material which could easily be replaced. In making the screen test for the picture I took a calculated risk.

When the day for my test came I played the wineshop scene as the director expected me to—quietly, with an undertone of bitterness. This was a fairly simple scene to play. The real test, I knew, would be the Tribunal scene.

I had thought about all that must have happened during the hate-maddened, blindly hysterical days following the fall of the Bastille. Wine kegs must have been smashed open for the peasants to get drunk on. I could see them marching through the streets, cursing their deposed enemies and shouting, "Down with the *aristos!*"

After the first part of the test had been completed, I hastened back to my dressing room, loosened the tidy black wig, plunged my hand into a jar of cold cream, then ran it through the hanging strands of hair. The cotton mobcap was replaced by the red cap of the Revolutionists, ornamented with the *tricolor* rosette. I was sure that Madame De Farge, like the other revolutionaries, had been roaming the streets, celebrating the downfall of the aristocratic order under which the French peasants had suffered so grievously. Her tidiness surely must have disappeared into limbo; on the wave of her hatred she would have resembled one of the Furies of whom the ancient Greeks made such powerful use.

I looked into the mirror at the transformation I was working on. My nails ripped into the fichu of the dress until it hung in shreds. As a final touch, I leaned down, swept my bare hand over the dusty floor, and in one stroke smeared my face and throat with the dirt I had gathered. I liked the result.

I went back to the placid little gentleman who was making my test. "Merciful Heavens!" he exclaimed. "You aren't going to look like *that!*" "Yes, I am," I answered quietly. "This is what Madame De Farge *would* look like by the time she leaps up on that Tribunal stand."

The director continued to protest, but I held my ground. He finally shrugged and said, "Well, honey, it's your funeral," and proceeded with the test.

Later, from Jack Conway, who directed *A Tale of Two Cities,* I had a first-hand account of the effectiveness of my experiment. He told me, "Dave Selznick and I had sat through all the previous tests for the part. Some were very good, but still Selznick was not satisfied. When that wild, maddened creature suddenly flashed onto the screen he jumped up, clapped me on the shoulder, and said, 'This is it, Jack. We've got it!' "

And that was that.

Which only goes to show that babes in the woods sometimes find the right path by instinct.

The Hollywood engagement of *A Tale of Two Cities* was a gay and diverting experience. It was a time (1934-35) when Hollywood "glamour" was at its peak, when ambitious hostesses vied with one another in arranging beautiful and extravagant parties. At the most popular restaurant of the day the luncheon hour presented a gathering of celebrities which thrilled me as well as the fans who stood at the entrance collecting autographs. Incidentally, my own promise to my nephews and nieces to bring back autographs of the famous movie stars was never fulfilled. I had bought a beautiful hand-tooled leather album for the purpose. But once I began meeting the celebrities I found myself oddly shy about asking for their signatures. The only "name" I brought back, which stands to this day in lonely splendor on the first page, was that of Freddie Bartholomew.

I am certain that the effectiveness of my characterization of Madame De Farge was due to the fact that she seemed to me not a conventional "heavy," but a creature who transcended her personal grievances to become the instrument of a people's vengeance. One must try to imagine the workings of such minds if one is to create more than a superficial, conventional characterization. Some inner identification, which even I cannot explain, has caused this to happen, particularly in the case of two parts I have interpreted: Therese De Farge and Gina Ekdahl in *The Wild Duck*. In both cases I immersed my imagination in the emotional life-patterns of these two exactly opposite types of women. They rewarded me richly.

It comes to this. The intangibles of acting are often achieved by serving the part and the play in ways of which the actor himself may not always be conscious. This is what you, the audience, remember long after the memory of the play itself may have grown dim.

What was hardest for me to learn in adjusting to camera techniques is the need for condensation of both voice and gesture. I have learned a great deal by watching emotional scenes being filmed at such a low pitch that I, standing a few feet away, could hardly hear what the actors were saying. Yet, when the scenes I had observed came on the screen, they had exactly the right degree of audibility.

I recall Basil Rathbone's description of an experience of his when playing with Greta Garbo in *Anna Karenina*. It was during a scene in the carriage when Anna and her husband, Count Karenin, are returning from a ball. The two have become estranged in their marital relations. The Count suspects the affair Anna is having with Count Vronsky, but he makes an attempt at a reconciliation. Anna receives her husband's advances without response.

In the filming of the scene, as far as Rathbone could

perceive, Garbo did absolutely nothing. Yet the director called, "Print it," and seemed pleased. The next day, when Rathbone saw the previous day's "takes," he realized how Garbo had reacted at the crucial moment. She had simply withdrawn into the far corner of the carriage, moving an infinitesimally small distance. By that one tiny movement, she conveyed Anna's shrinking physical aversion to the man she no longer loved.

In motion pictures a player has only to *think* himself into a part with complete concentration; the penetrating eye of the camera does the rest. Few gestures are needed; only the inevitable ones are believable. The actors on the screen seem as close to you in the audience as someone in your own living room. There is no need to strain to see or hear them. Everything looks real. Everything is detailed and accurate. Your imagination can loaf; the medium makes comparatively few demands upon it. On the other hand, of course, there are films that will move you deeply, and those you will not soon forget. By the process of the close-up and the focussing of his camera, a movie director can guide your attention to the point he is trying to make, holding it there as long as he sees fit. You have no choice in the matter; you have to look where he wants you to look. This results in a simplification of your own mental processes.

At a "live" play, your attention is more diffused; both the director and the actors have to reckon with this fact. While the good actor knows how to hold your attention, it is nevertheless true that your eye is free to wander where it will. A cat walking across the stage can ruin a scene for the finest actor in the world. Should a cat stroll across a movie set during the shooting of a scene, the director merely calls out, "Cut!," pussy is locked up, the same scene is shot all over again, with audiences none the wiser.

There are fashions in films just as there are in clothes or automobiles. Several decades ago, the favorite heroine had to be a cute little girl, preferably with long golden curls. The stage play, *Boy Meets Girl,* by Bella and Sam Spewack, spoofed this type. Then, with Theda Bara, Gloria Swanson, and Pola Negri, the *femme fatale* plot became popular. It reached its full flowering in the gaunt beauty of Greta Garbo. Her artistry is not dated. The restraint of her exquisite Camille makes her performance of the lovesick heroine as fresh and as touching as if it had been filmed today.

Few experiences are more enlightening than to see, after the passing of a few years, a movie which had once interested, even delighted us. I happened to catch a reshowing of *King Solomon's Mines* which, I seem to remember, received good notices when it was first released. You doubtless recall that this picture was the dramatization of H. Rider Haggard's story about a search for hidden diamond mines.

My second look at the film revealed two things: first, that the love story is that of Shakespeare's *Taming of the Shrew,* told in an African setting with Victorian costumes; and, second, that the hero, played by Stewart Granger, successfully woos his haughty lady, Deborah Kerr, without speaking a single word of love throughout the entire film! I sat through it twice to make sure of this. Not one term of endearment is exchanged between Stewart and Deborah, yet you know that they will "live happily ever after." On the screen looks are more important than lines.

In *King Solomon's Mines* the animal sequences brought back to me one of John Barrymore's wry comments: "Never try to act with a kid or a dog. They'll steal the show every time." That's just what happened. Those giraffes and zebras and rhinos tossed the actors right out of the window.

"Westerns" have been the mainstay of the movies since their earliest days. Galloping horses and cowboys, strong men, sometimes good, occasionally one gone bad, fighting, or refusing to fight—in saloons, in barns, or mountain passes—all this has long been favored fare for movie fans. The typical hero of these "horse operas" is usually patient, taciturn, quick on the draw—always tall, broad in the shoulder, slim of hip, and always able to ride, ride, ride!

Westerns have long been a boon to the movie box office whenever that institution goes through an occasional attack of the jitters. These Westerns have created the great American myth, one which is popular throughout the world, wherever American movies are shown. They provide their audiences an escape from the regimentation of modern life. They carry the imagination into the freedom of wide open spaces and show us courageous men struggling to bring the law to frontier towns where the man who was able to shoot first had once made his own law.

In the typical Western, womanhood, children, and animals are, for the most part, treated with respect—and the heroine is almost always a model of virtue and wisdom. Horses have their own special place in the hero's heart. Such traditions have always been the backbone of the Western film.

The advent of television has increased the popularity of the Western beyond all counting. Serials such as *Gunsmoke, Wyatt Earp, Wells Fargo*—to mention only a few —have created new popular idols. The devoted fans of James Arness, Hugh O'Brien, Dale Robertson, and others far outnumber those of the average matinee idols of stage or screen.

The Western story has gradually grown more complex; the simple conflict between the good man and the bad has expanded. Occasionally each recognizes worthy qualities in the other. With the filming of pictures such as *High Noon, Shane, The Treasure of The Sierra Madre,* and *Big Country,* material with psychological overtones and a more adult viewpoint has introduced new elements of interest. As time goes on, these elements will undoubtedly provide many a new twist to the routine Western plot. But whether these plots are simple or complex, I venture to say that Westerns will continue to make their perennial appeal to the vast public they have acquired since the first horse and rider galloped into view.

Music Marries Melpomene

Do you realize that a new form of entertainment has appeared in the theatre within your own lifetime? I am talking about the flood of "dramas with music" which are doing unprecedented business all over the country. They are adaptations of successful, often serious plays, which are now being set to music—music which may be called "popular," or, in any event, music which the producer, the author, and the composer hope to see listed on the hit parade.

There was charm in the old-fashioned musical, in which pretty girls and chorus boys sang and danced the chorus numbers; in which the young lovers were practically always chastely clad and had fair, often good, voices. They usually sang a couple of solos and, sooner or later, a duet in which June was rhymed with moon, and the phrase "I love you" was sung in varying degrees of frequency and fervency.

Usually a pair of comics supplied humor as a contrast to the sentimental story, and at the final curtain the entire cast would line up for the glorious finale. These musicals insured the customers a pleasant evening and had astonishingly long runs. *Floradora* ran sixty-three weeks on Broadway; *Oh Boy* ran for fifty-five performances.

In time a new note crept into these shows. Popular comedians began to graduate from the old-fashioned burlesque houses into musical comedy. Fanny Brice was one of the graduates. Burlesque was a great training ground for comedians. The most notable transformation in the career of an actor took place when David Belasco made a legitimate star of David Warfield, a Jewish comedian who was appearing in the Weber and Fields Music Hall burlesques and who became one of the most sensitive and beloved players of many generations. His appearance as Anton von Barwig in *The Music Master* by Charles Klein earned him a unique position in the hearts of the public. Warfield, unlike most actors, died a millionaire. The delightful Ina Claire began as a Follies girl and developed into one of the most sparkling feminine interpreters of high comedy on our modern stage.

A major milestone in telling a story with music was Jerome Kern's *Show Boat,* adapted from Edna Ferber's novel of the late twenties. Since its first production on Broadway in 1927, it has been revived twice on the stage and has also been filmed and refilmed. Jerome Kern's music is played and sung almost as much today as when it first enchanted the public of the thirties. Here was a musical with all the customary conventions—gay choruses and comic relief—but it also concerned itself with a very serious theme, the tragedy of miscegenation.

The forties marked the appearance of a surprising new type of hero. *Pal Joey*, based on John O'Hara's *New Yorker* stories, introduced an attractive "heel." It also introduced to fame a young dancer, Gene Kelly. Mr. Kelly has since become a motion picture star, a director and a choreographer of note. Surprisingly enough, the ruthless cynicism of *Pal Joey* made a tremendous hit with fun-loving musical comedy audiences. Its filming a decade later produced another surprise. Frank Sinatra, former crooner and idol of the hysterical bobby-sox set, proved in this picture that his serious acting talent, first displayed on the screen in *From Here to Eternity*, was no flash in the pan. Here was an actor.

Out of Tin Pan Alley came the genius of George Gershwin who elevated the standards of popular music in this field. Beginning with songs like *Embraceable You* (from *Girl Crazy*) and *The Man I Love* (from *Strike Up the Band*), he wrote music as alive today as when it was first composed. Lyrics, in the hands of his brother Ira, grew more sophisticated, polished, clever. Gershwin's serious music—*Rhapsody in Blue, Concerto in F,* and *An American in Paris*—won him international fame. He was the first composer of jazz to be heard in a concert at Carnegie Hall. Even today, almost thirty years later, the announcement of an all-Gershwin Night at the Lewisohn Stadium in New York always insures a sell-out.

But the crowning achievement of a career that was all too brief was his Negro opera, *Porgy and Bess,* based on the play by Dorothy and Du Bose Heyward. This opera has made history in the realm of international relations. Under the aegis of Robert Breen and Blevins Davis, it has entertained a worldwide audience and has made Gershwin's name known in far countries. On still another plane, the world tour of the all-Negro cast in the opera has done much to combat international misunderstanding.

As the treatment of "the book" increased in sophistication, even psycho-analysis was spotlighted as the theme of a musical comedy. Gertrude Lawrence's performance as the neurotic heroine of *Lady in the Dark* was one of her greatest triumphs. Her song, *The Saga of Jenny,* became an immediate hit. But the surprise sensation of the opening night was a new comedian named Danny Kaye. After the public had accepted and acclaimed *Pal Joey* and the ultra-modern *Lady in the Dark,* the old-fashioned musical was definitely dead to all intents and purposes.

With the production by the Theatre Guild of *Oklahoma!* in 1943, Richard Rodgers and Oscar Hammerstein II combined serious drama with unforgettable melodies and a new era dawned. Where hitherto music, with a few exceptions, had been linked with a slight and highly sentimental story, composers now began to seek more weighty material. In *Carousel,* Rodgers and Hammerstein went even further, blending hit tunes which are still being sung and whistled, with an adaptation of Ferenc Molnar's exquisitely sensitive play, *Liliom.*

South Pacific, based on James Michener's stories, set a new high in musical comedy. When the Rodgers and Hammerstein team wooed Ezio Pinza away from his career at the Metropolitan Opera, a new kind of masculine charm was injected into the musical comedy world. According to Joshua Logan, the producer of *South Pacific,* Mr. Pinza was a very frightened débutant in the new field. But audiences must have speedily cured him of his stage fright. The middle-aged charmer became a new masculine idol.

Just when one thought that success in the "drama with music" field had reached its zenith, *My Fair Lady* raised her pretty head. No Rodgers and Hammerstein opus this time. Allan Jay Lerner and Frederick Loewe turned the trick in making George Bernard Shaw's *Pygmalion* into an utterly enchanting entertainment, with a star who could not sing but most certainly could act, and a leading lady who could do both.

Creators of musicals have continued to delve further into the gold mine of serious material for plot ideas. Today's theatre-goer can see Sidney Howard's Pulitzer Prize drama, *They Knew What They Wanted,* all wrapped up in a superb musical score and renamed *The Most Happy Fella.* Even the grim power of Eugene O'Neill has made the transition from *Anna Christie* to *New Girl in Town.*

Long before this drastic alteration in pattern and style occurred in musical entertainment, the world of the dance had undergone startling changes. It is interesting to realize that four American women contributed to this metamorphosis.

Formal ballet had always thrived in Russia, and

throughout all Europe as well. Its devotees preserved a highly formalized art—an art quite as special in its own language of gesture and movement as that of the theatre of the Orient.

But, at the turn of the century, a courageous young American girl out in California boldly proclaimed a new doctrine of beauty. Our bodies, she insisted, like those of the ancient Greeks, must be liberated from the artificial restraints which ballet techniques imposed. Corsets, girdles, ballet shoes—all these must be discarded; they caused an unnatural distortion of the human figure. To Isadora Duncan they were anathema. In her credo the dance was not a diversion but an expression of life, the soul exercising itself through a free, vitalized body, through movements which stemmed from the rhythms of nature, from flowing lines of great sculpture, from the inspiration of noble music. She took her ideas to the cultural centers of Europe, where this slip of a girl was soon acclaimed as a new high priestess of the dance.

Isadora Duncan revolutionized the artistic world's concept of movement. She regarded the dance as a most important means of re-educating the human race. Her ideals must first be taught to very young children, she proclaimed. She even adopted a group of children to further this end and devoted many years to working with them, sharing the beauties which had been revealed to her.

As Isadora Duncan reawakened the public to the wonders of Hellenic art, so, somewhat later, Ruth St. Denis, another American woman, took the beauty of the

Oriental concept of movement out of the temples and art museums and brought it into the lives of the casual theatre patron. She appeared in vaudeville; she gave dance recitals. From Denishawn, the school founded by herself and her talented young husband, Ted Shawn, there presently emerged the steely, uncompromising power of Martha Graham, who went much further than her teachers in her tireless search for the beauty that is truth. To her thousands of emulators, and to her own special public, she is regarded as a great instructor as well as a superb artist. She, in her turn, has created a new concept of the dance. She uses the body as a fine actor uses his voice, fascinating the mind while the eyes follow patterns of movement which become beautiful because they are expressive.

Out of this kaleidoscope of styles there appeared in the thirties still another style, created by another American girl with a fresh viewpoint.

Agnes De Mille, niece of the great motion picture director, Cecil B. De Mille, had acquired her dance technique the hard way, of which rigorous ballet training was a part. It was she who introduced the fresh, gay Americana which characterized the dance patterns of the fantastically successful play, *Oklahoma!* Who can ever forget the vitality of her *Rodeo* number, and, in *Carousel,* her lovely, imaginative ballet on the beach? Her vivid sense of theatre, which is part of her heritage, makes her dance numbers an integral part of the action of the play.

In 1930, when *Lysistrata* reached the Broadway stage, after slumbering like a Sleeping Beauty for two thousand years, Doris Humphrey choreographed the *Bacchanale* which was the colorful climax at the end of the play. The dancing was dominated by a young male dancer with exceptional magnetism; his name was José Limón. Since that

91

time he has become an international figure, a giant in the field of the dance. His sensitive face, the purity of line through which his almost ascetic demeanor expresses itself, have all contributed to the progressive, expanding movement of the modern dance world. Other interesting figures have appeared in this ground swell of change, of which the end is not yet in sight.

And through it all exquisite interpreters of formal ballet continue to astound the world with their magnificent technique and their beautiful artistry.

In less pretentious types of dancing, the demands made upon performers have become more and more exacting. The girls and boys of the chorus are expected to demonstrate increasingly difficult dance steps, combined with the ability to speak an occasional line.

That show people often draw upon a variety of talents and exhibit great versatility is demonstrated in the delightful motion picture, *Indiscreet,* when Cary Grant, who began his stage career as a music hall song-and-dance man, draws upon this early training to do some nifty footwork. James Cagney, too, had his early training as a hoofer. Fred Astaire has combined a captivating talent for dancing with a charming gift for light comedy, first on the stage and then in pictures. Leslie Caron abandoned a promising career as a ballerina in Paris to become a wistful and charming motion picture actress in such films as *Lili* and *Gigi.*

In various areas of theatre, the dance is becoming increasingly meaningful and important. The sensational success of *West Side Story,* with its fresh choreographic patterns, is another example of a musical making use of a classic plot. I venture to say that ticket buyers who have stormed the box office have little realized they were begging to see, in *West Side Story*, a modern version, set to music, of Shakespeare's *Romeo and Juliet*.

As far as musicals are concerned, there *is* something "new under the sun."

You Too Can Be a Critic

T HERE IS A GENERAL rumour abroad that actors hate critics. In the popular mind there seems to exist an impression that there is perennially a pretty war going on between these two, a kind of unspoken distaste for each other's very existence.

In all honesty I cannot subscribe to this myth. I have an almost unwholesome respect for the opinions of certain astute, erudite, and eminently fair critics to whose comments I have been forced to submit from time to time.

Seriously, I have learned a great deal from these gentlemen of the press who, on opening nights, constitute a Supreme Court of Judgment from whose verdict there is rarely a successful appeal.

Personally, I believe this is unfortunate. One reads with envy, in books written by European repertory actors, of the recovery in later performances of acting values lost in the throes of first-night insecurity. But in our theatre, with very rare exceptions, the fate of a play depends upon the impression it makes on its opening night.

If the majority of the critics damn a play, the chance of it being seen by an out-of-town audience is practically nil. As part of that out-of-town audience your opportunity of being able to render your own verdict as to whether a play is to your taste is never given you.

Movie critics do not seem to have this same power. Both motion pictures and television have brought into prominence reviewers of unusually high calibre and discriminating tastes. Nonetheless, a movie, in spite of devastating reviews in the metropolitan newspapers, may play to impressive grosses all over the world. Apparently the motion picture public makes up its own mind and maintains its own brand of loyalty to its favorite players.

But to return to the stage attractions. The condemnation of the critics is not, of course, the only reason you do not see Broadway plays and musicals if you live, for instance, in the Midwest. In addition to the fact that only smash hits survive in New York, the economic problems of touring a company are so formidable that only the producer of a sure-fire attraction can take the risks involved.

On the other hand, in countless instances the condemnation of the critics is justified. They have to sit through many a play which should never have been produced in the first place. They perform a public service in assisting its demise.

Professional critics are simply those who have concentrated their attention on the theatre and have learned to express themselves clearly and succinctly. They too, oddly enough, are human beings (though some actors may dispute this) with eyes, ears, and powers of observation with which you also are blessed. But the critic has become an informed person, either through sheer exposure to the theatre or through following the bent of his natural curiosity in his chosen field. Probably you have no intention of being a professional critic yourself, but you can learn to bring the qualities of a trained critic into the theatre with you if you will. Ideally speaking, the purpose of criticism should be to evaluate how successfully the author's concept has been expressed by him and how successfully the actors have interpreted that concept. Beyond this it becomes a question of how much the critic and you have liked the subject matter presented. Your own ability to appraise a play or a performance will be enhanced if you learn to look for these two concepts.

If you can separate the player from the part in your mind's eye, you will have progressed a great deal. Of course a really clever artist won't permit you to do this. He can make *his* way of playing a part seem the only right way, and we are willing to forgive the worker of such magic.

An intelligent actor accepts criticism with grace provided he is not being made the victim of a wisecrack. Sheldon Cheney, in his book, *The Art Theatre,* has this to say on the subject: "There are far too many reviewers with a show-off complex. A facility for clever writing betrays them."

The perceptive faculty which I hope you will develop will enable you to recognize the sort of verbal buffoonery which for a few years passed for criticism. Happily, this style of reviewing has been largely replaced by a more thoughtful and literate kind of appraisal.

In their turn, actors must learn to accept criticism honestly made and to benefit by it. It is dangerous to sit in one's ivory tower marinating the ego. Actors must be sensitive, but the ego is one part of their psyche which they cannot permit to be easily bruised.

Never hesitate to write to an actor, giving him your frank opinion, pro or con. But remember that very few workers in the theatre are entirely free to choose their own material. You must remember, too, that no artist can always turn out a masterpiece. (In the theatre we call a smash hit a masterpiece.) You must also remember when you attend a performance of a play you have not seen before that you yourself are, in effect, a first-nighter. You have the same privilege of judging what you see as has the professional critic. You should come with no preconceived notions. The trouble is that all too often you do come with preconceived opinions based on what your favorite critic has said about a play, a picture, or a TV show. Unfortunately, most people know all too little about what they are seeing or hearing.

One of the reasons why baseball is so popular is because people *do* know a lot about it. They know the box scores of their favorite players; they know whether they are hitting well this season as compared to last. To be sure, you and I can go to a baseball game without knowing these things. We can even get a lot of pleasure out of just watching. One cheers with the crowd merely because excitement is contagious. But if you know the rules, the fine points of the game, if you can recognize a foul ball, a good pitch—if you can appreciate great skill when you see it—in short, if you know what is going on, you can have a far better time than if you don't.

What makes you applaud—or yawn—when you see a play? Why do you get a great deal from some plays and little or nothing from others?

In a world where you have movies and television as well as live drama, you probably see more entertainment than a dozen critics reviewing plays nightly would have seen twenty-five years ago. But how much do you know about what you are seeing and listening to? Do you simply like or dislike, accept or reject? One performance may prompt you to say, "That was swell." To another your reaction may be, "That's terrible! Turn it off!" Rarely do you say, even to yourself, "That was good because . . ." or, "It would have been better if. . . ." You may not get much nor retain much of what you have seen and heard. But if you do know what is behind the work of your favorite performers as well as you may know the techniques of your favorite ball players your perception will be keener, your judgment more accurate, and, most important of all, you will have a better time.

Theatre isn't like any other art form, which can exist alone, unseen or unheard. A masterpiece of painting can hang in a gallery, loftily indifferent as to whether you see it or not. It can afford to wait. A great book can collect dust on the library shelf; it too can wait. But an actor's performance cannot wait. In its very essence it is living communication. Its life is of the moment and then it is gone. Gone, except for the effect it has had on you.

I enjoy immensely reading critical reviews written many years ago concerning performances given by the great ones before they were great. Some seventy or eighty years ago, the work of individual artists in the theatre was dissected and analyzed in great detail in the public prints. We do not have much of this kind of detailed analysis today. The review of a play must appear in our daily press immediately after the play opens. And it must be fairly brief because of limitations of space. (However, expansions of these reviews in Sunday editions often contain deeply thoughtful analyses.)

In the magazines and newspapers of even two or three decades ago, one could read highly literate criticisms from men like Stark Young, the late George Jean Nathan, and, greatest of them all, in my opinion, H. T. Parker, who reviewed plays for the now defunct Boston *Transcript*. These men wrote critiques from which a performer could learn much, especially when they regarded one's work unfavorably. It is important for an artist who has failed to please not only to know that he has failed, but to learn the reasons why.

Back in the eighties dramatic criticisms contained keenly comparative analyses of artists whom we have come, with the passage of time, to think of as always having been immune to criticism. Seeing them only in the light of their recognized eminence as we do, these analyses made in a former day are very revealing. For example, you can read, in Arthur Row's biography of Bernhardt, *Sarah the Divine,* what the great French critic, Francisque Sarcey, had to say of Bernhardt's early performances: "She has no stage presence." Another critic: "She has no personality, only a voice."

Henry James complained of her lack of technique, of

her "reliance on the eccentricities of her personality." One wonders what would happen in our entertainment world of today if such "reliance" should become tabu! In our theatre whole reputations have been built on personality alone.

The focus of criticism today has largely shifted from the player to the play. Actually, this is a good thing. It places the emphasis where it belongs. No longer do playwrights manufacture tailor-made "vehicles" designed to fit the limitations of some popular star of the moment. Of course playwrights naturally have certain actors in mind while they are writing. One can readily understand this. But the best of modern playwrights try to put into their work an idea which takes possession of them, and to realize the vision which, for the time being, fills their imaginations. Even more than in Shakespeare's time, "the play's the thing."

The metropolitan critics, however, are prone to judge every play offered on the basis of its appeal to the sometimes overly sophisticated tastes of the Broadway habituées. But there is a public that enjoys and would support far less sophisticated entertainment. This may well be true not only of the out-of-town public which seldom gets to Broadway, but of a numerically important public living within the five boroughs of New York.

An example of a play that survived, despite the coldness of the New York critics, was one in which Walter Huston starred. It was called *The Apple of His Eye*. It was a simple story in which Mr. Huston's warm sincerity and folksy charm found grateful expression. It was dismissed by the critics in a series of not too helpful reviews.

Fortunately, Walter Huston was in a position to do something about it. He accepted the critics' verdict and bowed out of the Broadway picture. Then, counting on his movie following, he took the play on tour, playing to what were apparently contented audiences for the remainder of the season. Such plays have a right to live, and audiences the right to see them. It is a mistake to ignore their needs.

But what about you in your role of critic? Whether you are seeing a stage play, a movie, or a television drama your critical sense and your power of selectivity can establish the standards to which those who cater to you must sooner or later measure up. But first you must possess knowledge enough to distinguish between the good, the bad, and the merely mediocre.

The other day I saw a play about which I could not make up my mind. I was puzzled, for it was a great popular success; yet I left the theatre dissatisfied. I tried to ask myself a few specific questions in an effort to clarify my impressions. You might put them to yourself the next time you see a play which particularly interests—or puzzles—you.

1 *What is the play about? Answer in a brief sentence.*

2 *How well has the author told his story?*

3 *Does the subject matter seem worth while to you?*

4 *Have the actors, supporting players as well as stars, successfully conveyed to you the author's intent?*

5 *Is the physical production realistic or imaginative? Would you say that it is inadequate, good, or superb?*

6 *How did the audience seem to respond to the play? How much were you influenced by the comments of people in the lobby between the acts?*

7 *Could you, without reading any reviews, urge your friends to see the play? Do you take the trouble to do this after seeing a play you like?*

8 *Would your interest in a given play lead you to search out and read other plays by the same author?*

The Power and the Glory

WHAT IS THE element of magic that makes a performance "great," whether you are seeing it on the stage, on the screen, or on television? The creative process which goes into fine acting is so individual and so intangible that it seems almost impossible to define. Nevertheless, I shall try to show you how some artists work, in the hope that in doing so I may give you an increased sense of participation and illuminate your own experience as part of an audience.

Your pleasure in watching any performance will be enhanced by knowing something about the resources upon which the artist draws. I will try to indicate at least some of the paths all of us travel before we can show you what may appear to be simple results. You can scarcely be expected to realize the many experiments of trial and error through which performances that please you must evolve. Occasionally, by some happy accident, a player clicks unusually early in his career in a part which fits his personality like a glove. Overnight he may become a star. He can travel all his life on the wave of that early success. But gradually he may cease to try to do anything beyond exploiting the tricks of personality from which his earliest success has stemmed. There are many such performers. Often they grow rich and very popular, but nonetheless they have failed to make full use of the talents with which they are endowed.

One cannot blame these individuals, the rewards of personality worship being what they are. Nevertheless, when you have seen them, through repetition, become a stencil of themselves, you leave the theatre vaguely dissatisfied—without quite knowing why.

On the other hand, there are actors who, by means of endless striving, become craftsmen who thrill you because of the versatility of their talents. They make you remember their work long after lesser performers are forgotten. Early in the century Richard Mansfield, a distinguished star of those days, made his début when a very young man as the lecherous, shaky old Baron Chevrial in a trivial play called *A Parisian Romance*. He went on to give outstanding performances as Richard III, Beau Brummell, and Peer Gynt. His was a perfect example of a type of career in which, season by season, he expanded his range.

Bette Davis has shown more courage than most artists in refusing to conform to the stereotyped standards of acting and of beauty which tend to prevail on the screen. Her freedom from convention in this regard has resulted in some of her finest performances. She has never been afraid of playing unsympathetic roles provided they offer her the opportunity to do a fine characterization.

Modern audiences tend in great part to be personality-worshippers. They go to see so-and-so playing this-or-that in such-and-such—in just that order. It is the pull of the actor that may draw you into the theatre quite as much as the desire to see the play. And you may see excellent acting, but when this happens the part is submerged in the actor. When he plays himself, with slight variations, to be sure, I call this "personality acting."

An example of an actor whose range is unquestionably wider than the roles which have become his trademark is Charles Boyer. One is told that on the stage in Paris he played many kinds of parts, yet in America so completely has he become identified with the deep-voiced *homme fatal* roles that he is seldom permitted to use any other facet of his talents. When he showed us in the concert reading of Shaw's *Don Juan in Hell* how much more he could do, one can only regret that he has been so rigidly type-cast on the screen.

We have a striking instance of the fullest use of a great gift in Laurence Olivier. The young Englishman who was first seen in this country as the colorless bridegroom in Noel Coward's *Private Lives,* and who, a little later, played the petulant husband with Katharine Cornell, in *No Time for Comedy,* has grown immensely in stature through the years. Today, as an internationally famous actor-director, he has made a distinguished contribution to theatre history with his *Henry V,* his *Oedipus Rex,* and his *Richard III.* Yet, with amazing range, he was able to tickle our funny-bones with his Justice Shallow and the absurd Mr. Puff in Sheridan's lampoon of theatre people, *The Critic.*

One may be very sure that over the intervening years he has never stopped working at the perfecting of his craftsmanship. In so doing, he has brought these diverse characters into the life of your imagination, making of them people you feel you know.

I myself had always felt a certain indifference to King Oedipus and his tragic problems. I shared, to some extent, John van Druten's opinion expressed in his book, *Playwright at Work:*

> When I saw Oedipus not long ago, I could not resist a feeling of deep impatience. I wanted to say, "Oh, do stop bothering yourself so! You couldn't help it. . . . The circumstances were dead against you. It's unfortunate but you needn't go on like that about it."

But I was to change my mind when Olivier revealed the power and the pathos of the play. In it he uttered a cry of animal agony which can never be forgotten by anyone who heard it. He achieved a remarkable effect of massiveness and dignity by means of a costume trimmed with broad horizontal stripes. The make-up of his eyes, chin, mouth, were designed to broaden his features, thereby giving weight and importance to his appearance.

Olivier played *Oedipus* as the first half of a double bill. In the second play on the program, he underwent a startling transformation. When he walked on as the ludicrous dandy, Mr. Puff, in *The Critic,* his entire appearance had an upsweep. *Everything*—his coat tails, his periwig, even his nose—turned up. The contrast between the two performances was almost incredible.

It does not follow that an actor is always successful in his attempts to escape from the limitations imposed upon him by type-casting. Some fine artists have foundered on the rocks of public indifference to their laudable ambitions.

Alla Nazimova "failed" when she tried to put imagination and real drama (as opposed to the "reel" variety) into the movies of her day. She was willing to pay for her faith in her ideals by using her own money in her experiments. An unquenchable idealist, she produced and played Ibsen on the stage when to do so was a far greater gamble than it came to be later. Her pioneering efforts paved the way for the subsequent public acceptance of Ibsen plays as entertainment.

Nazimova relinquished her own stardom to join the Civic Repertory Company, an organization in which Eva LeGallienne, single-handed, gave to America for seven years the kind of repertory theatre which is enjoyed by almost every important city abroad. It was with this company that Nazimova gave her extraordinary performance in Chekhov's *The Cherry Orchard.*

Jane Cowl "failed" when she followed her notable success as Juliet with equally beautiful productions of Maeterlinck's *Pelléas and Mélisande* and of Shakespeare's *Antony and Cleopatra.* She hoped to build a repertory with those three plays. It was her intention to tour the country with them, and into the project she poured the considerable fortune she had earned in popular plays like *The Gamblers, Within the Law, Lilac Time,* and *Smilin' Through.* But her public, after having flocked to see her Juliet, was indifferent to her Mélisande and Cleopatra. She was forced to return to the more popular type of play out of which her earlier successes had been built. But her Juliet placed her among the immortals of our theatre.

Eva LeGallienne "failed" to establish permanently her Civic Repertory Theatre which operated on Fourteenth Street in New York at prices easily within reach of everybody. Single-handed, and with heroic courage, she produced, in repertory, plays of distinguished quality which might otherwise not have been seen. Such a repertory theatre, committed to a policy of low prices, must be subsidized. After the financial crash of 1929, wealthy patrons of the arts became hard to find. So the Civic Repertory closed its doors.

It is such "failures" as these which are among the glories of our theatre history.

Whether you are aware of it or not, you, the audience, have certain basic requirements when watching a performance. These requirements are actually very simple. You want to become emotionally involved in the play. You want to feel with the characters. The more you can identify yourself with what you are seeing, the more reality it will have for you.

A funny situation is funnier if you can imagine yourself either as part of it, or superior to it, or if something of the same nature has happened to you. The same thing holds true if the situation is serious or tragic. Of course you need not have undergone the identical experience.

Let us say, for instance, that you are watching a picture showing a desperado pursued by the law. You need never have been in his boots, but you probably have some idea of how it would feel to be hunted. The movie must do the rest—must enable you to feel with and understand the gunman on the run. Then, through your own ability to imagine how it feels to be hunted, you will identify yourself with the story. If the movie failed to help you understand the emotions of the bandit—if you haven't the vaguest idea of how it would be to run for your life—then you will care little about what is happening on the screen and the movie and its characters will leave you cold.

When you make the necessary identification your understanding of people, places, and periods increases automatically. So of course you grow. At the end of the play your horizons of thought and feeling have expanded, your understanding of human nature has increased.

I myself had a curiously illustrative experience in this regard.

Some years ago I was sitting quietly studying in my hotel bedroom in Minneapolis. I had been brought to that city to appear as guest star in three Ibsen plays. The play that week was *A Doll's House,* a play which shed a new light on marriage relationships. Presently my telephone rang. I lifted the receiver to hear a strange woman's voice. "You do not know me, Miss Yurka, nor do I mean to intrude upon you, but last evening you brought about a change in my life for which I simply have to thank you. It's like this: my marriage has been gradually nearing the rocks. Because of family interference my husband and I were growing farther and farther apart. Last night, after seeing what happened to those two people in the play, we sat until dawn discussing our married life together with a new understanding of each other. I believe our marriage is saved. I simply had to call you to tell you this —and to thank you."

That was all. We hung up. I sat there in the winter sunshine which was coming through my hotel window, thinking. My mind was filled with wonder. Once again the magical thing had happened. Nearly a hundred years ago an angry little man in Norway tossed a brickbat into the theatre hothouse of his day when he wrote a play about a doll-wife who rebelled against her own ignorance of moral values. He changed the world's thinking about the relationship of men and women in marriage. As one writer put it, "The slam of the door behind her as Nora left her home echoed around the world." How odd that these many decades later, in an American city in the Midwest, far from Ibsen's homeland, a woman was thanking him for what he had done.

What is the process by which a characterization is achieved? I have been asked many times how I go about the creation of a new part, what "method" I use. How I wish I could answer in a few brilliant, succinct, and illuminating sentences! But any attempt at theorizing goes flying out of the window when I remember how my Gina Ekdahl in *The Wild Duck* came into being.

To begin with, I was not particularly impressed with the part as an acting opportunity. A drab housewife who had been a servant before her marriage to her photographer husband, she had no great scenes in which to seize the audience's attention. Four other parts in the play are more effectively written. As rehearsals progressed, I be-

110

came more and more absorbed in watching those other parts develop. I was fascinated by the characterizations the other actors were building. There seemed little for me to do other than to fit my lines honestly and modestly into the wonderful tapestry of human nature and its quirks which Ibsen had woven.

Suddenly I found that I knew my lines without having made any real effort to memorize them. And those lines took their inflections and their emphases from what the other players were doing. I do not know whether it would be safe to risk working in this way with a playwright of lesser genius than Ibsen. But with Gina Ekdahl it worked.

When it came to playing Ibsen's Hedda Gabler, it was quite a different matter. Hedda is a cerebral and highly neurotic character—an introvert who has a sardonic streak of heartless cruelty, which, at the time the play was written, made her seem a monster. It is interesting to note that today her brand of humor is not only accepted but has actually become popular. It makes up much of today's conversational badinage.

I had to approach Hedda with a good deal of imagination. My chief interest in attempting her was my feeling that she should be played (particularly in the first two acts) for much more comedy than I had ever seen done, and that as much light charm as possible should be injected into her early scenes. After all, "General Gabler's beautiful daughter" had been a reigning belle. Left penniless after her father's death, she had married, for lack of a better offer, George Tessman, a dull, pedantic scholar with a limited income. Her distaste for him and for her lowered social status had made her a neurotic, frustrated woman. Married to another type of man—above all a man

111

of means—she might have become a brilliant hostess and a reasonably contented woman. Unsympathetic as Hedda's character undoubtedly is, the part has challenged the talents of a great many actresses.

In my turn, I tried, with the use of a good many calculated effects, to show new facets of the role which, it seemed to me, had not always been brought out. It was a fascinating assignment.

Ellida, the heroine of *The Lady from the Sea,* was for me the most difficult of any of the Ibsen roles I have played. Ellida is replete with Northern mysticism. Her longing for the sea is linked to her obsession with "the Stranger," a seaman to whom she had pledged her troth, only to have him disappear immediately afterward. When he turns up again, years after she has married a kindly, understanding doctor from the "inland country," her agony of conflict is finally resolved in a scene which I, for one, found virtually unplayable.

The fault lies at the door of Ibsen himself. In my opinion, he resolves the major problem presented in the play so abruptly that the final scene is unbelievable. It was not only in my own performance that I felt this. My reaction was identical when I saw two other interpretations. I was not convinced.

I believe my performance of Gina, the most successful of my Ibsen characterizations, was instinctively based on my mother's personality. All sorts of memory impressions help one to characterize—impressions that have been received and stored away unconsciously among the millions we accumulate in the course of any twenty-four hours. An actor's inner ear is a recording machine which he constantly uses, even when he is unaware of doing so.

There are many intangibles involved in both playwriting and acting—intangibles that are the result of the genes with which one is born.

When it is possible to do so, a player likes to test his versatility—to flex his acting muscles, so to speak—in another kind of part than the ones with which he is usually identified. We saw this when Laurence Olivier stepped away from the royalty roles (Richard III, Oedipus, *et al.*) which had lifted him to the upper rungs of the theatrical ladder, to play the sleazy, down-at-the-heel vaudevillian, whose humor as well as behavior were thoroughly disreputable, in John Osborne's *The Entertainer*. For Olivier to adjust his distinguished abilities to such a characterization was no mean feat—whether one liked the subject matter of the play or not.

My own desire for a change of pace was fulfilled when I was allowed to play the lead in *Spring in Autumn*, by the Spanish playwright, Martinez Sierra. (His delicate little play, *The Romantic Young Lady*, is a popular piece in the repertory of almost every little theatre.)

Spring in Autumn was a fairly amusing study of a temperamental prima donna who, having given up family life for her career, returns home for a brief visit to assist in the marriage plans of her seventeen-year-old daughter.

In our production, her tantrums and her antics culminated in a bit of business (injected into the play and *not* in the original script) wherein I did a Yoga headstand and, from that position, sang the first four bars of *Vissi d'arte* from *La Tosca!*

In his review of *Spring in Autumn*, Robert Benchley wrote of my acrobatic feat, "If that won't bring you into the theatre, nothing will."

Nothing did. The "temperamental prima donna"

theme was outworn, and we closed in six weeks. But I had a wonderful time playing comedy for a change.

Training for and in our American theatre has, in the past few decades, undergone revolutionary changes. These stem from the excitement caused by the first visit to this country of the Moscow Art Theatre company in 1923. The use of Constantin Stanislavsky's books on his methods of acting and producing has spread to almost every college drama class, to every drama school, throughout these United States. The word "Method," and the concept of training it projects, has been so carelessly bandied about that one hesitates to further belabor the subject. However, so important have been the results of putting into practise Stanislavsky's ideas that one cannot possibly ignore this development. In 1898, Stanislavsky gathered around him a number of his friends who were putting on plays. Their combined efforts and their dedication to his ideals eventuated, over a period of some twenty-five years, in ensemble playing of the highest order. (Incidentally, it may interest you to know that as a result of the visit of this distinguished and by then highly professional company to this country, the mildly idiotic custom which prevailed on the American stage at the time—that of actors taking curtain calls at the end of each act—was dropped and has never been resumed. Our whole standard of acting was elevated to new heights.)

Those members of the Moscow Art Theatre company who elected to remain in this country at the end of the engagement, began to teach theories of acting which, while interesting in themselves, can be dangerous to inexperienced practitioners in the theatre. I would almost say that only a fairly experienced actor, one who unconsciously has been practising many of the precepts of this great Russian teacher, can fully benefit by the study of Stanislavsky's theories.

During my own visit to Moscow in 1934 I was fortunate enough to hear from Stanislavsky's own lips some illuminating comments. He was aware, he said, of the fact that our American theatre practices—our casual assembling of players who may never have laid eyes on one another before, our necessity of making a smash hit on an opening night, and, failing that, of finding the theatre dark a few days later—all these factors, he admitted, did not permit of the kind of deep probing, of continuous experimenting, which the members of his permanent companies enjoyed. His book, *My Life in Art,* he told me, was not so much an effort to tell others how to learn the art of acting as it was an effort to describe "how *we* have learned to act in twenty-five years of collaborative effort."

One dedicated attempt to put into practise the Stanislavsky theories was made by a number of people who, later, called themselves the Group Theatre. Organized in the early thirties, under the inspired leadership of Harold Clurman, Lee Strasberg, and others, these individuals approached their purpose very seriously. For a period of some ten years they searched not only for the inner content of the plays they produced, but for the meaning of the society for which they were producing them. Their approach was a refreshing change from the plays designed primarily for box-office appeal. The Group Theatre stimulated the imaginations of its followers and a more thoughtful attitude on the part of both players and audience developed.

Two especially distinguished talents emerged from

the efforts of the Group to establish a new kind of theatre: the dynamic playwright, Clifford Odets, and the actor and director, Elia Kazan. The power and craftsmanship of Kazan's directing have vitalized the whole American theatre scene.

Unquestionably, the value of Stanislavsky's books is inestimable. But I have seen a great deal of bad acting, heard a deal of non-productive theorizing, by young people whose smattering of information culled from these books has actually interfered with their natural talents. They have become bogged down in a confusion of ideas— ideas which can only be assimilated and utilized through years of practice.

To be sure, any practice routine which makes one work at a craft is infinitely better in the theatre than no practice at all. It is also better than confining one's acting to a routine repetition eight times a week of a small, un-demanding part in a hit play. It is during the run of such plays that the player has, for the time being, security and leisure of which he often makes little intelligent use. Therefore, the movement, now well established in New York, of drawing together ambitious players who wish to experiment with their talents, can, and already has, pro-duced some impressive results. Under the guidance of a distinguished director, these actors meet regularly to do scenes from plays or to improvise on a theme. Their work is then subjected to the criticisms and comments of the remainder of the group who serve as audience. Several highly gifted young players have emerged from this group effort.

Nevertheless, in my lifetime I have seen much magic projected by players who work by methods of their own which bear no relation to our gifted and highly articulate visitors from across the Baltic Sea. Helen Hayes is one of these. Shirley Booth is another. Noel Coward has certainly evolved a method of his own and so, I suspect, has Fredric March. The necessary equipment for an acting career can be described in a very few words. There is no substitute for talent, of course. But even talent must acquire a vital, coordinated body and a vital, disciplined speaking voice, then must place them both at the service of the imagination. For without all of these, all the theories in the world will not produce that magic in a performance which is what you, dear audience, go to the theatre to see and to enjoy.

There are, of course, many individuals who give you pleasure who simply work at acting as they would at any trade. They want to earn a living. If the talent is first-rate and the player has gone through the mill, doing all sorts of parts, both good and bad, he surprises everyone when a real opportunity comes his way. The acting equipment, the techniques are all there, polished and ready. Assuredly the results of Shirley Booth's long experience in the radio show, *Duffy's Tavern,* must have contributed a good deal to the effortless charm she brings to her comedy roles and to the touching pathos she evoked in *Come Back, Little Sheba* on both stage and screen.

I believe I could never have essayed the *Electra* of Sophocles when opportunity offered had I not played countless parts in stock, and had I not, years before, developed my voice and my diction as part of my training to become a singer, which was my earliest ambition. The vocal power had been lying dormant, waiting to be used.

117

There are a few players who seem incapable of giving a bad performance. John Barrymore was one. What he was like in his very earliest days I do not know. But by the time I was able to afford to see him on the stage he had become so deft in his comedy roles, so romantic in such plays as *Peter Ibbetson* and *The Jest,* so sinister as Richard III, and of course so unforgettable as Hamlet, that my memory is filled with impressions of beauty and craftsmanship of the highest order.

Paul Muni is another actor who never fails his audience. His early training in the Jewish theatres on the Lower East Side in New York laid the groundwork for his superb characterizations later on the Broadway stage and on the screen. His portrait of the famous trial lawyer, Clarence Darrow (*Inherit the Wind*), hangs in my sparsely filled gallery of great ones.

Few actresses have been as completely satisfying as was Katharine Cornell in Besier's *The Barretts of Wimpole Street.* Hers is a remarkable gift for evoking an aura of beauty and romance. It made her Juliet memorable.

Julie Harris, among the younger stars, seems to be handling her career with intelligence and a lofty ambition to identify herself with the best. Her fragile appearance, combined with her sensitivity and sophisticated humor, are harbingers of an exciting future. She, like Miss Cornell, is aware of the importance of audiences away from New York and is building up her following by touring whenever possible.

It is in the field of stark tragedy that we find a dearth of great players. To be truly effective in tragedy one must not be afraid to risk being savage, electric, even ugly if the part calls for it. It is the very essence of tragedy that it be larger than life, that its power to move you be like some great force of nature which you cannot resist. It overwhelms you. And unless players are willing to risk being thought savage and ugly and—well, titanic—let them leave tragedy alone. A much better living will be assured them if they do.

I happened to recall passages from a book written by Sommerville Storey about the great sculptor, Rodin. I quote Mr. Storey: "He [Rodin] would not admit the existence of ugliness in nature." Storey goes on to quote Rodin himself: "That which one commonly calls ugliness in nature may, in art, become great beauty. It is simply the power of character which makes beauty in art; it often happens that the more a creature is ugly in nature, the more beautiful it is in art. In art only those things that are characterless are ugly; such have no beauty, exterior or interior. For the artist worthy of the name, all is beautiful in nature because his eyes, boldly accepting all truth shown outwardly, read the inner truth. . . . That which is ugly in art is that which is false and artificial . . . that which aims at being pretty or even beautiful."

On the other hand, the passion for underplaying can wreck a powerful play. As an example, Strindberg's *The Father,* one of the most soul-searing dramas of modern times, must be ruthlessly realized if the power of the play is to be felt. No understatement of the bitterness with which Strindberg drew his characters is permissible. To skirt the ugliness implicit in this masterpiece is to defeat the intention of Strindberg when he wrote it.

George Arliss, a most engaging actor in the field of satiric comedy during the early twenties, made his greatest success in Louis Parker's *Disraeli.* But when he attempted

Shylock in *The Merchant of Venice* he failed, in my opinion, because his characterization had no vibrations of hatred in it. In the play Shylock speaks of having been spat upon by the Christians. Mr. Arliss was far too much of a gentleman for anyone to be able to believe that this could be done to him, not even as the sadistic moneylender of Shakespeare's play.

My admiration for Helen Hayes is boundless. In *Coquette* and in *Victoria Regina*, she gave remarkably clever interpretations. When she played Mary Stuart in Maxwell Anderson's *Mary of Scotland*, she met a great challenge. If we are to believe history, Mary was a tall, passionate woman, capable of risking all for love. Through the sheer authority of her performance Miss Hayes succeeded in convincing both critics and public that she *was* Mary Stuart, despite the totally different qualities with which she had hitherto charmed her audiences. It is in the meeting of such a challenge that an actress grows in stature.

Not long ago, I picked up a volume of critical essays, *The Scenic Art,* by Henry James, in which he describes his impressions of the Paris stage in the late eighties. He speaks of a young actress of "limited talent . . . her only asset her charming voice . . . all personality, little or no technique. . . . Will not go far." The name of this young actress was Mlle Sarah Bernhardt.

Costumes and make-up are invaluable aids to the actor. For instance, Sarah Bernhardt was actually of small physique, not at all the imposing figure she appeared to be. But she knew how to manipulate draperies, and, being a painter herself, she designed costumes which, on the stage, made her seem tall and majestically proportioned. In her photographs you will note that she is prone to pose on the steps of a throne, a long scarf trailing far below the level on which she stands. If she wore a crown (as in Sardou's *Theodora*), it would be an unusually high one, making her seem tall and queenly in spite of her less-than-average height.

Acting is such an intangible, evanescent form of expression that you should give it the full meed of appreciation at the moment of your response to its evocative power. For that is the only moment in which the actor's art is really alive. No one can tell you exactly what Booth's Hamlet was like or define the secret of Maude Adams' elfin charm as Peter Pan or as Babbie in Barrie's *The Little Minister*. Today, we respond to Mary Martin's gay vitality, to Marilyn Monroe's satirical sexiness, to Marlon Brando's persuasive masculinity—though the real secret of their particular charm continues to elude one.

Sometimes we witness the evaporation of the magic which has made a reputation. There may have been mannerisms of voice or of personality which added charm to the fires of talent, even of genius, while these were burning brightly. But as the fires die down, or are banked, the mannerisms become increasingly evident instead of being lost in the radiance as they had been previously. It is then that one begins to question whether one had always worshipped a bag of tricks. But this is not true. The tricks are merely more noticeable once the glow of the original gift has grown less bright.

I know that the first time I saw Sarah Bernhardt—it was in *Madame X*—I suffered a great disappointment in the early acts. I felt that she had been overrated, that she had been over-publicized through a kind of Barnumlike publicity campaign. Her highly stylized use of her voice, her mannerisms of gesture, seemed to me unnatural and distracting. It was not until she reached the famous court-room scene toward the end of the play that a surge of feeling came across the footlights. It was only then that I saw a flash of her power.

It is conceivable of course that in her almost endlessly repeated farewell tours, Bernhardt may have spared herself in her less important scenes, saving her fullest energy for the climactic moments which her years of experience had proven would by themselves sustain her great reputation.

The contrasting talents of Sarah Bernhardt and Eleanora Duse have had so many books and articles written about them that my own comments could not fail to be redundant. Besides, I saw the two women only at the end of their very long careers. Each in her prime must have been a fascinating creature to have inspired such worldwide adulation. Indeed, the brief motion picture record of Duse, which is periodically shown at the Museum of Modern Art in New York, is as modern in its restrained beauty as if it had been made today. Unfortunately, the film of Bernhardt on the same program is so badly done, and her movements and gestures are so jerky, that it does great injustice to her reputation as an artist.

It was not until her final "farewell," at the Empire Theatre in New York, that I was caught up at last in the web of magic Bernhardt had spun over most of the world for so many years. I went to see her almost with reluctance. The amputation of a leg had of course restricted her to a very few scenes. I was afraid that the disappointment I had experienced once before might be repeated.

The first part of the evening justified my apprehension. Here were only the remnants of greatness. The voice still echoed its famous music (she was in her late seventies), but it was a weary woman we were watching, struggling against what seemed hopeless odds.

The final scene on the program of excerpts was the death scene from *La Dame aux Camélias,* or, as it has always been called in English, *Camille.* The curtain rose on the dimly lighted bedroom of the dying courtesan. The nurse lifted her from her pillows. My breath caught. It was as though some great hand had wiped away forty years from that strangely fascinating face so that those of us who had missed her in her prime might have one final glimpse of a glorious gift. This was no aged actress trading on the sympathy of a devoted public. This was a woman dying of love who looked ill only because she was dying and knew it. And when the actor who played the young lover, Armand, came running in, eager to claim once more the woman he had discarded, it was a young, passionate creature who fell into his arms and prayed for life. We longed to see her love once more fulfilled. And when her limp arm told us she was dead it seemed an almost unbearable sorrow.

The audience broke into a frenzy of applause when the short scene ended. And I, the doubter, almost the scoffer when I came into the theatre, left it after midnight, my eyes drenched in tears, my hands clutching three large photographs of "Madame" which I had stopped in the lobby to buy. I have them still.

Because of that half-hour's glimpse of her greatness, it distresses me to hear at the Museum the howls of laughter with which certain young people greet the pathetic little piece of celluloid on which her acting has been recorded. There is derisive laughter, too, at some of the early Garbo films made before the techniques of film acting had been modulated to their present restraint and naturalness. Too bad.

On this same program Duse emerges quietly from a dark shawl in which she has almost concealed herself, to show us a face ravaged by sorrow, framed in white hair, but of such an unearthly beauty of line and expression that, as in all her movements in the film, the glory of the ancient Greeks seems incarnate before your eyes.

I saw her in her entire repertory the year she died, pitifully, in a cold, strange, American city. My memories of her are among my dearest treasures.

I came away from seeing Duse with a new concept of acting, with an impression of a purity that had shed all tricks, all the dross with which so many of us sometimes compromise. Only truth was left and it was more than enough.

When I think of her I seem to see an alabaster lamp with a soft white light burning inside it. As an actress, I am glad to have lived in a world through which a Bernhardt and a Duse have passed.

Today we have another great Italian in our midst, and while she is of "the earth earthy," and evokes no such aura as did La Duse, Anna Magnani has her own magic to which I succumb. She too has a kind of heightened life force of her own. I should like to see her playing one of the great roles, in her mother tongue, in which her rich, volatile talent could have full play.

We have our own wonder people in this country. Marlon Brando could do anything he'd a mind to, if he'd put his mind to it. Katharine Hepburn keeps her tryst with the theatre every so often and I believe has yet to reach her zenith as an actress. She is not afraid of being called a character actress long before she need be. (As though all good parts are not "character parts" if the player plays them honestly.)

Spencer Tracy is almost unbelievably believable. I've never seen him make one false move nor strike one false note.

But there is danger in a too-constant adherence of any actor to the medium of the screen alone. Two fine players whose talents became constricted because of the limited range permitted by the screen were Ronald Colman and Leslie Howard. Despite the "Oscar" Mr. Colman won for his performance in *A Double Life,* it was one of his lesser achievements. I consider his Sidney Carton in *A Tale of Two Cities* a finer piece of acting. Had he been able to alternate his screen impersonations with an occasional tour of duty on the stage, he might have played the *Othello* sequences in *A Double Life* more convincingly.

Leslie Howard's *Hamlet* failed for similar reasons. For all its visual beauty (and his appearance alone should have made him a dream Hamlet) the general effect was one of timidity and over-restraint. Had he shown the wisdom of Katharine Cornell when she tackled *Juliet*—had he, as she did, toured the country for an entire season, adjusting his Hamlet to auditoriums of changing size and audiences of varying tempers before facing his ultimate board of judgment on Broadway—I believe he would have had a triumphant success in the part. The constant closeness of camera and microphone on the movie set calls for a reduction in volume of voice and a limitation of movement and gesture which, transplanted to the open stage, make an actor ineffective. These were what defeated Howard as Hamlet.

To no one has the theatre yielded its rewards in greater measure than to Alfred Lunt and Lynn Fontanne. If one were to try to visualize an ideal career surely it would be one such as these two charming people have enjoyed. They have taken infinite pains to keep their standards of acting at top level. No compromises seem ever to have been made, except in one department—their choice of plays. All too rarely have they identified themselves with great literature. Not that they have not occasionally done a fine play. Robert E. Sherwood's *There Shall Be No Night* had dignity and depth. I rank it among the Lunts' best efforts. Giraudoux's *Amphitryon* was a masterpiece of satiric spoofing, and their madly farcical *Taming of the Shrew* was gloriously funny. They have appeared in many other plays, of course, but these three seem to stand out as being especially worthy of their superb talents.

In the spring of 1958 they appeared in Dürrenmatt's ugly and powerful play, *The Visit*. This is a play about appalling human greed and unrelenting hatred. The Lunts showed genuine courage in tackling it. It is a risky business to depart from the formula by use of which popularity has always been assured. But their public seemed to respond with enthusiasm.

No one wants to court failure, but there are times when, if one is to be true to his star, one must risk it, unmesmerized by fear.

As a rule, you can trust an artist. If he has pleased you heretofore give him your support when he goes a-venturing now and then. There are a few artists who never let you down. Seek them out; follow them. It is a loyalty which pays off. Only by your following them as they reach toward wider horizons can they continue to grow in artistic stature.

So really it all comes back to you, doesn't it? You too must risk something in the pursuit of the courageous and the true. The integrity of an artist is his highest gift. But there must be the integrity of the audience as well. And what do I mean by "integrity" of an audience? I mean that you, as well as the artist, must follow your highest ideals, constantly seeking to repudiate the meretricious or the merely slick. You must prove to the artist that you are willing to follow him—and that you are counting on him to lead you to heights.

Very Truly Yours

WELL, DEAR AUDIENCE, it's time to bring this book to a close. Inevitably, there still remains so much unexplored territory, so much more I'd like to say to you. But theatre, like life, is inexhaustible, and, like life, to be meaningful it must be experienced instead of talked about. If any of the things I've told you in these pages have sharpened your interest and helped to increase your enjoyment of theatre in general; if you view the plays you see in the future—on the stage, on motion picture and television screen—with a more discerning eye because you know a bit more about how they "got that way"; if, in short, I've helped to make your play-going more fun, I shall be satisfied.

And above all, if I've succeeded in whetting your appetite for *better* theatre, through whatever medium it comes to you, then indeed I am doubly satisfied.

For, once again, it is necessary to put the matter of better theatre right into your collective laps. If you do want better "live" theatre and more of it; if you are one of the many thousands in this country who seldom (perhaps never) see stage plays performed by professional companies and devoutly wish that you could; if you feel that there are all too few first-rate movies and far too many third-rate ones; if you are sometimes heard to moan over the current state of television and to sigh for more mature dramatic shows of top-notch quality—then I say to you, "Speak up." For it is truly up to you to demand what you want, to make your voice heard. Believe it or not, the kind of theatre which we will have in the future, no matter through what media it is presented, depends not only upon the gifts of the playwrights, the talents of the performers, the perspicacity and pursestrings of producers and managers, distributors and booking agents. It depends largely upon *your* tastes—and your willingness to express those tastes by shunning what you *don't* want and shouting for what you do.

Not that you will get what you want—in the quality and quantity you want it—overnight. Far from it; we both know that. But there *are* things you can do to help bring live professional theatre to communities far from Broadway. (I've indicated some of the things in the informational section at the end of this book.) And, as I've said now and again in preceding chapters, you can make your opinions felt, register your approval or disapproval of the movies and TV shows you are getting, by telling the men who make them—and your local movie-house or TV-station manager as well—what you honestly think, backed up by knowledgeable reasons for why you think it.

To want the best—at every level of your life—is your inalienable right. And theatre, in its highest meaning, is a rich heritage, bequeathed to you by the ages. The theatre I am talking about is the theatre of the titan Greeks, of Shakespeare's "infinite variety." It includes the charm and cynicism of the eighteenth century; the witty word-games of Wilde and Shaw; Ibsen's iconoclastic hammer-blows at the social evils of his time; the theatre of Sir James Barrie and Arthur Miller, of George Kaufman and Tennessee Williams; of William Inge, Lillian Hellman and Thornton Wilder; the monumental theatre of Eugene O'Neill, revealing America to the world in terms of courageous, powerful thinking. All, all of these and many others, have contributed to the theatre which is your birthright.

To bring to any aesthetic experience enough knowledge to be able to appreciate its finest values is to increase enjoyment a hundredfold.

Our minds and hearts can meet through this living, breathing art. And if, through the pages of this book, you have come to share with me my enthusiasm for the best there is of the past and the present, as well as my dreams for the future—if I have helped you ever so little to do this— then I and my beloved theatre can happily sign ourselves,

VERY TRULY YOURS

A Miscellany
of Assorted Information
for Playgoers

EVERYWHERE in America theatre is undergoing a revolutionary change. In New York the drama critics are reviewing off-Broadway productions on a regular basis. "Reading recitals," in which dramatic material is presented, sometimes by one artist, sometimes by several, are touring the country and are proving to be immensely popular with an astonishing diversity of audiences. Such distinguished players as John Gielgud, the celebrated English actor, our own Katharine Cornell, and Charles Laughton, have scored notable successes with this form of entertainment.

I myself, when presenting my own one-woman program—from Maine to Texas and from Florida to Hawaii—have had the opportunity to observe at first hand many of the changes taking place throughout the nation, and to note the broadening expansion of taste on the part of the American public in general.

At Stratford, Connecticut, something new has been added to the American theatre scene. The Stratford Memorial Theatre is presenting Shakespeare, played by

Americans, as an *annual* summer festival event. Its Shakespearean productions bring into prominence many interesting players who show us new facets of their talents.

Federal sponsorship of the dramatic arts is being seriously considered and advocated in important places . . . All of these are but a few of the significant portents of change.

Television is gradually (though as yet all too infrequently) bringing into our homes some of the finest, most exciting talent to be found in the entertainment world. Movies, new and old, keep vividly before us the charms of many players whom we love and have loved in the past, while "top-drawer" producers for Broadway continue to gamble astronomical sums of money on plays and musicals in the hope that they may reap equally astronomical returns. Thus the *status quo* is being maintained; but at the same time everywhere things are slowly, sometimes almost imperceptibly, changing.

Across the length and breadth of the land, "live" theatre is taking on new ways of doing things; more and more, it is stimulating the talents and abilities of all sorts of individuals who, in one way or another, want to be "part of the act."

Off Broadway. In New York the 1950's have witnessed the mushrooming of what has come to be known as off-Broadway theatre. Night after night, winter and summer, uptown and downtown and in obscure side streets, off-Broadway houses present a variety of theatre fare—classics of both the distant and the recent past, experimental dramas staged in experimental ways, new works by hitherto unknown young playwrights. Off-Broadway productions provide an important channel for professional actors (both veterans and newcomers) to expand their range, and to be seen by "uptown" critics and producers as well as by the theatre-going public. Off-Broadway management is coping with the need for lower production costs which make possible a reduction in the price of tickets, thus bringing live plays within range of the average person's budget.

Throughout the Land. In San Francisco and Seattle, in Dallas and Oklahoma City, in Cleveland and Milwaukee, from Coral Gables, Florida, to Cambridge, Massachusetts—on West Coast and East Coast and in the middle of America—we find community theatres flourishing, in different forms and by many different means.* Some of these theatres use professional talent only; others put on plays with casts composed entirely of amateurs; still others use a combination of professional and amateur actors.

College and university theatre productions are legion. The drama departments in hundreds of institutions of higher learning put on an astonishingly wide variety of plays—and not only during the academic year. Many blossom forth with successful summer festival seasons as well.

The physical structures which house the community theatres of today appear to be almost as varied as the fare these theatres present. They range all the way from charming, well-equipped buildings, designed expressly for the purpose they are intended to serve, to arena stages which may be set up in any available space. (It is this arena-style staging, by the way, which has brought the term "theatre-in-the-round" into our vocabulary.)

We find community theatres thriving in converted barns, vacant restaurants, old factories, abandoned

---

* For the sake of brevity and to eliminate confusion, the term "community theatre" is used here *chiefly* to denote non-professional and semi-professional theatre (with the obvious exception of college and university theatre).

churches, or even, in one instance, in a former brewery. Americans have learned that it's fun to "get into the act" —whether that means the donning of grease paint, painting of scenery backstage, or helping in a subscription campaign.

Community Play Houses Help Keep Theatre Alive

The story of the vigorous growth and development of the community theatre movement in America adds an important chapter to the cultural history of our country. It is the devoted efforts of non-professional groups—made up, as they so often are, of "the butcher, the baker, the candlestick-maker," of stage-struck young people, housewives, bankers, lawyers, scientists, or what-you-will—that have kept alive the habit of theatre-going in the United States. Outside of our metropolitan centers, they have for decades provided thousands of Americans with their only live theatrical diet. From the most modest of beginnings, many of these amateur groups have evolved into full-fledged professional companies which frequently invite noted guest stars to participate in their productions. But large or small, amateur or professional, they contribute living theatre to the communities in which they function.

Obviously it is impossible here, in so limited a space, to discuss, let alone attempt to describe, the accomplishments of the many community theatres which are thriving in cities large and small from coast to coast. One can at best pay only the briefest tribute to a few individuals whose resourcefulness, unflagging energy, determination and unselfishness of purpose are representative of the spirit that motivates hundreds of leaders in the community theatre field. One of its far-seeing pioneers, of course, was the late Margo Jones whose theatre in Dallas was one of the first of its kind to attract nationwide attention. Public-spirited individuals like Mary John who established in Milwaukee a permanent professional company financed by the dimes and dollars of Milwaukee citizens—from taxi-drivers to bank presidents—make outstanding contributions to community life. Milwaukee's Miller Theatre now belongs, in a very real sense, to every member of its theatre-minded public.

Two community theatres which have combined student actors with professional guest artists are the beautiful Pasadena Community Play House in California, and the Cleveland Playhouse in Cleveland, Ohio. Operating the full twelve months of each year, Pasadena's director, Gilmor Brown, has produced an unusually distinguished roster of plays. In Cleveland Frederick McConnell has developed a really unique plant which is a genuine civic asset. The Playhouse consists of *two* theatres—one for plays of broad general appeal, the other, and smaller one, devoted to dramas of an experimental nature.

In 1958 The Cleveland Playhouse was selected by the Ford Foundation as a base from which to launch a highly important experiment. With costs underwritten by the Foundation, a professional touring company is being trained for a specific purpose. The players who make up the company are to undergo two years of intensive work at the Playhouse; then, in the third year, they will tour a cross-section of cities and towns in the Midwest. Audience reaction will be carefully studied in order to draw valid conclusions as to whether or not the people of this area would really *want* live theatre if it were made available to them regularly at reasonable prices. Findings from this study will undoubtedly have significant implications for the entire country.

Educational Theatre in America

Nowhere else in the world have colleges and universities fostered theatre as have our own institutions of higher learning. More than 400 American colleges and universities produce at least three plays annually; 70 of these have modern theatres equal, or superior, to professional Broadway houses. These do an average of from six to eight productions during each academic year.

The drama department of Antioch College in Yellow Springs, Ohio, serves as a splendid example of the high standards, the ingenuity and energy, which characterize educational theatres in the United States. Under the able direction of Arthur Lithgow, for five summer seasons Antioch presented Shakespeare's *entire* dramatic works— a practically unparalleled achievement!

There is a wealth of material dealing solely with community and collegiate theatre. Dozens of books, magazine articles and pamphlets describe past and present work in this field. (You'll find some of the books and pamphlets listed on pages 151, 161.

The Need for Resident Professional Theatre

Unquestionably, amateur theatres have contributed immeasurably to the communities in which they function. However, there seems to be a steadily growing conviction among theatre lovers that, in a country as rich as ours, we should be able to endow a chain of live professional theatres—theatres with standards of production which would place them on a par with the art galleries, symphony orchestras, and public libraries of which we in these United States are so justly proud.

Like the citizens of other nations throughout the world, surely Americans have a right to enjoy permanent, professional companies which would bring them the best which live theatre has to offer. Without any doubt, talent in this country is unlimited. Each year the drama departments of colleges and universities graduate hundreds of gifted young people who have devoted four years of serious study to theatre. And this study has included all phases of the dramatic arts—production and direction, for example, as well as acting. But the Broadway stage, television, and the motion picture industry absorb only a fraction of this fresh talent. Most of the young folk, then, must bury their abilities—and the knowledge and training they've acquired—in other occupations, or teach other young people theatre techniques for which there is no appreciable market. What a pity! And not only is this trained, though yet untried, talent wasted through lack of theatrical activity; there are also literally thousands of individuals who have long proved what they can do when given opportunity. Many of these already possess distinguished reputations but their gifts must also lie idle—and for the same reason. To sum up, these artists have no chance to perform for you, and so *you* are deprived of a world of enjoyment which they would so gladly bring to you.

Kenneth Tynan, knowledgeable British drama critic, writing in *The New Yorker* Magazine in 1959, makes this statement:

> The American theatre is alive with talent, most of which, culturally speaking, is marking time. None of it is employed as it ought to be—in permanent companies where it might try its hand at everything from Aeschylus to Axelrod and grow by constant use. By a bizarre paradox, the barely competent performers do far more theatrical work than the most strikingly gifted; prestige deters the latter from taking artistic risks that might land them in a flop, while conscience forbids them to indulge in the kind of *kitsch* that would guarantee a hit. From the directors' point of view as well as the actors', there is not much doubt that the healthiest theatres are those

of Sweden, Russia and Germany . . . It is not that the grass grows greener there, but that it is more systematically nourished.

In the same article Mr. Tynan points out that, had we a state theatre, Marlon Brando might have played thirty "live" roles in ten years instead of only one. Of course this same thing can be said of dozens of other gifted actors.

Anyone deeply concerned with this problem is well aware of the obstacles that stand in the way of presenting professional theatre to the nation at large—and on anything like a year-round basis. Only occasionally, they realize, can Broadway producers afford to tour first-class offerings to smaller cities and towns; geographically our country is too large, and the financial expense of doing so is usually prohibitive.

Where Is the Answer?

Many believe that the solution to the problem is simply this: As is the case in almost all the other civilized countries of the world, we too must one day have a subsidized theatre. If small nations like Holland and Denmark have them, it is argued, why can't we?

There Is Something You Can Do

There is much that you, as an individual, can do to foster and support living theatre. You can become better informed about what is already being done. You can learn the pro's and con's concerning subsidized theatre, and what such theatre could mean to you if, for example, we could enjoy it in regional centers throughout the country. With only a little effort you can keep abreast of developments in this direction. And, if you do believe that a subsidized theatre is the answer to our needs, you can play your part by helping the individuals and organizations striving to bring such a theatre into being.·

The following pages describe sources of information on many subjects that are certain to be of interest to you. You will find descriptions of national organizations which will welcome your support, and which, in turn, can help you to become a more knowledgeable, a more active theatre devotee.

ANTA Belongs to You

The American National Theatre and Academy, familiarly known as ANTA, is an organization of theatre services, of information, and of other related activities. Anyone interested in the theatre may join. It is possible that you have not been aware until now that such an organization exists. But ANTA does belong to you, to all of us, in a very real sense, by virtue of the fact that it has been chartered by the Congress of the United States, and is dedicated to one purpose:

". . . to extend the living theatre beyond its present limitations by bringing the best in theatre to every State in the Union."

ANTA's beginnings, its early struggle to survive, its growth and the development of its potential for service and accomplishment, make a fascinating story, one with which you will surely wish to be familiar.

In the Beginning . . .

Here then, told very briefly, is the way in which the American National Theatre and Academy came into being. It was during the early thirties that two remarkable women, Mary Stewart French and Amory Hare Hutchinson, began to gather around them a group of interested individuals, all of them distinguished leaders in various fields of the arts, who were willing to lend their names to a national theatre project.

I have always been glad that I too had a hand in the early beginnings of ANTA. Circumstances made it possible for me to spark the interest of a gentleman in public life who was to prove an invaluable ally at a crucial stage in the crusade for government sanction of a National Theatre Foundation.

My part in the story came about in this way. In 1934, when I was returning from a tour of theatre festivals in Europe, I had opportunity to share my enthusiasm for the wonderful things I had witnessed with a fellow passenger on shipboard, the late Senator Robert Wagner of New York. His interest in the cultural welfare of his country made him a ready listener to my glowing account. I am afraid I walked the poor Senator around and around the deck endlessly—but I wanted to make certain that I had imbedded my ideas securely in his consciousness! I pointed out to him the discrepancy between our national wealth and the poverty-stricken façade which we present to other countries in regard to theatre. I could see that the Senator was impressed.

When Mary French and Amory Hutchinson decided that the time was ripe to tackle Washington as the next important move in their National Theatre campaign, I gave them a letter of introduction to the Senator. Here at last, I told him in my letter, was a solution to the need of which I had spoken, a concrete effort to remedy a serious lack in our nation's cultural life. I asked him to help the cause in any way he could.

Undaunted by a summer of appalling heat, which was tempered only by the coldness of their reception by the Congressmen who must be won over to the support of the project, the two women proved hard to defeat. With Senator Wagner's guidance, they did a masterly job of lobbying. Under pressure of their unremitting efforts, the interest of influential citizens and important Congressional figures in Washington was aroused so successfully that the path to the White House itself was soon opened.

On July 5, 1935, over the signatures of the President of the United States, the Vice-President, and the Speaker of the House of Representatives, a Federal Government Charter was granted and the American National Theatre and Academy became a reality.

A Federal Charter is not granted lightly, nor can a few sentences convey an adequate idea of the effort which went into its achievement. But the securing of a charter was only the first step on a long and difficult road. There was one particularly serious handicap—the granting of the Charter unfortunately carried with it *no Federal grant of funds* with which to implement its purpose. It was only through contributions of individuals whose personal resources permitted, and by means of the annual dues paid by its membership (a very small one in the beginning)— only through the devotion of voluntary workers during those early years—that ANTA was able to launch those activities which now constitute such an impressive chapter in the annals of the American theatre.

Early Efforts. For a number of years ANTA's progress was slow. As I have said, the lack of financial subsidy by the Government meant that getting under way presented enormous difficulties. To launch a drive for members requires funds, as does the maintenance of a suitable headquarters and a staff to do the necessary work. Yet somehow ANTA's first Board of Directors did find a path through endless financial and other problems, maintaining their courage and keeping their vision bright. Somehow, the all-important, all-necessary groundwork was laid.

WPA Theatre and the War Years. Throughout those early years, ANTA's main support came from the voluntary, unpaid labors of its tireless devotees who managed, through some very grim, dark days, to make the organization function. As always, a truly great idea eventually finds its own sources of strength.

Barely had ANTA acquired a set of by-laws and actually opened for business when the Federal Theatre was established by the Government as an emergency measure during the prolonged Depression which had descended upon the country. (Although the primary purpose of the WPA Theatre was to keep theatre people housed and fed during those lean days of the thirties, several of its achievements were notable.) During this period ANTA was forced to mark time. By the time the WPA theatres closed down, World War II was upon us. The Government was feeding the actors, all right—this time in uniform!

ANTA Begins to Function. But both depression and war ended eventually, and by 1946 ANTA's dormant years were a thing of the past. ANTA was now able to embark upon a program of really constructive action. Under the stimulating leadership of such individuals as Robert Breen and Robert Porterfield, and under the presidencies of Vinton Freedly, Helen Hayes, Robert Sherwood, and many other important figures, membership in ANTA increased and its activities and services began to expand. The successful organizing of Chapter One, the Greater New York Chapter, under the leadership of Virginia Inness-Brown, touched off the organization of other ANTA chapters throughout the nation.

As of today, ANTA's membership extends into every state in the Union, and its list of services—to amateur groups, to professionals, and to interested individuals—is truly impressive.

In order to fulfill its basic purpose—that of "bringing

the best in live theatre to every state in the Union"—the leaders of ANTA have worked indefatigably toward the formation of ANTA chapters from coast to coast. As its present Executive Director, Willard Swire, has stated in a brochure describing ANTA's activities, "If ANTA is to live up to its claim of being a national organization, it must create local cohesiveness and local activity . . . The Chapters fulfill this function. They bring together the theatre-loving people of a given community, molding them into a working entity; moreover, they create the means for the all-important regional exchange of ideas as well . . . If the growth of these Chapters continues, the National Office of ANTA will become what it should be—a coordinating factor, a consultant, a service body, and guide." (The brochure from which the above is quoted is called *The ANTA Story*. Beautifully illustrated with photographs, it is an exciting account of ANTA's achievement record—in much more detail than can be given here—in its attempts to bring the living theatre to all America. A copy of *The ANTA Story* can be obtained by writing to ANTA Headquarters, 1545 Broadway, New York, N. Y. You'll find it both fascinating and informative.)

ANTA's Achievements—A Partial Record

Once again, space limitations prevent one from giving an adequate picture of ANTA's present-day activities. However, here is a brief outline, in capsule form, of its services, and of some of the projects it has created, sponsored, or helped to promote, both in this country and abroad.

1. With funds raised by subscription, ANTA produced what was known as the *Experimental Theatre Series*

(1946-1949). The plays in the Series were of unusual character and value—plays which commercial theatre managers would not take the risk of producing. The *Experimental Theatre* introduced dramas by both new and veteran playwrights, on low budgets and for limited runs. The Series provided showcases for unconventional casting, and introduced several important new playwrights to the public. (Later on, ANTA carried the original Experimental Series even further, under the title, *"Invitational Series."*)

2. Beginning in 1948, and for several succeeding seasons, ANTA produced annually a brilliant variety show, *The ANTA Album*. Prominent stars donated their services—recreating, for one glamorous night, the roles that had made them famous. Thus, playgoers were able to see a nostalgic arc of the theatre of the past, as well as to greet budding new stars of the future. To make sure that the enjoyment of this unusual gathering of talent was not confined to New York audiences alone, a closed-circuit telecast of *The Album* was given, in 1955, to 40 cities from coast to coast. ANTA plans to continue production of the *Album* from time to time.

3. In 1954 a serious attempt was made to present outstanding American artists to audiences in other countries. This was done, partially by a small government subsidy, and partially through the contributions of internationally minded individuals. For example, under ANTA's sponsorship, *Medea* was presented at the West Berlin Drama Festival; Thornton Wilder's *The Skin of Our Teeth* was given as the "Salute to France" in Paris. The European touring productions of *Oklahoma!* and of *Porgy and Bess* stirred world-wide enthusiasm, especially since the all-Negro cast of *Porgy and Bess* presented the American Negro artist to the world in a new light.

In 1956, Congress voted to turn these sporadic emergency efforts into a permanent activity of the State De-

144

partment, under the title, "The President's Special International Program for Cultural Presentations." ANTA was appointed as the agency to administer this program, which includes not only theatre productions, but also jazz bands, symphony orchestras, solo artists, and dance ensembles, such as those of Martha Graham and José Limón.

To represent the United States abroad, in 1957 Fredric March and Florence Eldridge transported Eugene O'Neill's *Long Day's Journey Into Night* to France, presenting it at the Paris Festival of that year.

And during the same year a group of players which included Clarence Derwent, president of ANTA, Blanche Yurka and Margaret Phillips journeyed to Greece to open the Athens Drama Festival. In honor of author Edith Hamilton, they presented her translation of Aeschylus' *Prometheus Bound* at the 2,000-year-old Herod Atticus Theatre.

All of these activities are calculated to give the rest of the world a new conception of the best in America's cultural development.

4. ANTA's *National Theatre Service Department:* This Department offers to individuals and groups throughout these United States information which is invaluable. It provides an amazingly wide selection of services, such as:

> *Information Service:* From extensive files maintained and kept up to date at ANTA Headquarters in New York, this service answers questions about production and other problems sent in by any theatre group, professional or amateur. Questions may range from, "Where can I purchase second-hand lighting equipment?" and "Where can I buy a trick knife to use in *Dial M for Murder?*", to "How can I get Marilyn Monroe to come to our town to star in our production of *A Doll's House?*" Requests for a bibliography on

Children's Theatre, or for information on tax liability for a non-profit community theatre, for example, are carefully answered. Through its publications, through letters and telephone calls—as well as through personal interviews—the resources of this department of ANTA are available to all who need help and who ask for it. Members can get information about fund raising, budgeting, and publicity methods. Much of this information is already in published form; a list of its service publications is available without charge to any ANTA member who requests it. (Non-members may secure these publications for a nominal fee by writing to ANTA headquarters.)

5. ANTA operates a *Placement Office*—a clearinghouse of job information which furnishes community theatres, stock and resident theatres information regarding qualified personnel available for a multiplicity of jobs. This information is drawn from extensive files, kept strictly up to date, concerning directors, technicians, designers, actors, instructors, and others who may be looking for opportunities to work with community, educational, or professional theatres.

6. *Guest Artists Program*. In cooperation with Actors' Equity Association, this unique service makes available the talents of professional actors, directors, and lecturers for appearances with local community and university or college productions. Some of the guest artists attend regional conferences and meetings. Working within the local theatre's budget, ANTA handles all the required negotiations.

College students and community theatre companies find new stimulation in working with the professional artist, the publicity value of whose name not only pays dividends at the box office, but also serves to focus civic attention on the work of the local theatre.

7. ANTA offers a *Script Information Service* which lists play publishers and sources of special material. This department also supplies information concerning available plays, their agents, royalty rates, etc.

8. *Photographic Loan Service:* From its ample files, containing carefully selected representative photographs from productions on and off Broadway, from community, college, and children's theatres, and from summer and winter stock, ANTA lends, on request (and without charge), pictures for use in exhibits, for research, for classroom study, and for other worthy purposes.

ANTA's Future Is Up to You

I have tried to give at least a sketchy picture of what ANTA stands for, how the organization came into being, what it does for the public that loves theatre, and for theatre as an art. Above all, I want to re-emphasize the fact that, because it *is* an organization chartered by your Government, in a very real sense ANTA *does* belong to you. With support from you, as ANTA moves into the future its already expanding services and activities can open up new and wider horizons, and can give you an American theatre of which you may well be as proud as most Americans are reported to be of their baseball teams, their plumbing, and the modern American motor car.

It is heartening indeed to know that ANTA has plans for such a theatre in what is called "The Forty-Theatre Circuit Plan."

What Is This Forty-Theatre Plan? With the aid of

expert advice, ANTA officials have drawn up an extensive plan for the creation of *a chain of regional theatres*. These theatres would be strategically located in forty cities throughout the United States. Their goal would be to offer, on a year-round basis, professional live theatre of the highest possible calibre.

Of course such an undertaking would require intensive participation on the part of enthusiastic supporters. If enough such supporters would give concrete evidence of their earnest desire for living theatre, it is hoped that a Government subsidy for such an undertaking might eventually be forthcoming. It is also believed that additional financial assistance might come from some of the philanthropic foundations, several of which have already indicated interest in the American theatre scene. As an example of this interest, it is gratifying to note that, in 1959, the Ford Foundation made individual grants to eight new American playwrights. These grants, totalling $110,000, guarantee a first-class production of each writer's play in one of eight different cities. This in itself can surely be regarded as a "straw in the wind," and an encouraging portent of things to come.

Membership in ANTA. Wherever you live, be it in any one of our fifty states, you can become a member of ANTA. You can join as an individual or as part of a group. Either type of membership will make available to you many services, as well as all of ANTA's many publications—most of them without charge. And annual dues in ANTA are exceedingly reasonable. For full information and for a membership application form, simply write to:

ANTA Headquarters
1545 Broadway
New York 36, N. Y.

Other Organizations for the Advancement of "Live" Theatre

Council of the Living Theatre. The membership of this organization includes some of the most realistic minds in the producing end of the American theatre scene. The organization is made up of managers of theatres, not only on Broadway but in communities as far apart as Denver and Toronto. Through the Council, these men are searching for a formula which will enable them to bring to you, with the assurance of your support, the plays and the talents which have proved worthy of that support. They are earnestly looking for ways and means by which to rebuild "the road"—and to revive in the American public the kind of interest in live theatre which, once upon a time, made road shows both possible and profitable.

The Council is eager for public support and would be very glad to have your opinions as well as any ideas on this general subject. Write to the headquarters of the Council, 137 West 48th Street, New York, N. Y.

The League of New York Theatres is composed, in large part, of the membership of the *Council of the Living Theatre,* but it also includes theatre owners and others with affiliated interest. (Both these organizations maintain headquarters at the same address.)

The American Theatre Society. Throughout the country the Society has built up organized audiences for attractions which are sponsored by the Theatre Guild. The Guild's stamp of approval of course insures offerings of high quality. The Theatre Guild-American Theatre Society, founded in 1932, has for 27 years successfully organized and maintained subscription audiences in various cities in the United States and Canada, thereby, providing substantial guarantees to touring companies. In establishing regular theatre-going as a habit among its 120,000 subscribers in 22 cities, the organization has helped to stabilize the hazardous business of touring a show, and has been an important force in keeping "the road" alive. Members subscribe for a series of from four to ten plays (the number varies from city to city), selected from the best Broadway attractions. All professional plays of merit are eligible to be included in the play series. To accomplish the myriad details of enrollment, collection, seating, servicing, and local promotion, an office is maintained in each city, with a staff headed by a subscription manager. In New York, the Theatre Guild Headquarters staff, at 27 West 53 Street, handles the intricate problems pertaining to play selection, contracting for the attractions, national promotion, and the servicing of subscribers by mailing some two million dollars' worth of theatre tickets annually.

The American Educational Theatre Association. For 22 years the American Educational Theatre Association has been a great force in giving theatre its proper place in our American society. Founded in 1936, today the Association is the largest theatre organization of its kind in America, perhaps in the world.

Its more than 4,000 members represent nearly all of the 1,833 colleges and universities which offer courses in theatre. It also has many members from both community and professional theatre. The Association is governed by its officers and a Board of Directors. Fifteen of the Board members are elected by the membership; 18 members are appointed by national theatre organizations in order that the work of these organizations may be coordinated with the work of the Association.

AETA's year-round work program is conducted by 34 Presidential Committees; it has 23 permanent projects. These projects include many areas, ranging from Art Museums and Theatre Liaison, Audio-Visual Aids, and

College Curriculum, to Theatre Architecture and the Translation and Publication of Rare Theatre Books.

The Association's annual conventions bring together what is probably the greatest yearly concentration of theatre authorities to be found in the United States.

The International Theatre Institute. This organization was founded in 1948 by a group of international theatre leaders called together by UNESCO in pursuance of a policy of assistance to international organizations in the field of education and culture. The purpose of the Institute is "to promote the international exchange of knowledge and practise of theatre arts." There are thirty-three International Theatre Institute Centers in the world. ANTA is the United States' Center and is directed by Rosamond Gilder.

A List of ANTA Publications

(Available from ANTA Headquarters, 1545 Broadway, New York City—as of January, 1959. Additional pamphlets and other material are issued on a variety of subjects, in direct response to the need for such materials.)

The ANTA Story
An illustrated brochure describing history and activities of
    ANTA

Arena Theatre—1957: A Bibliography (compiled by Randolph
    Goodman)

Basic Technical Bibliography (compiled by Joel Rubin)

Blueprint for Summer Theatre and Supplements 1949-1954
    (written by Richard Beckhard and John Effrat), Price: $1.50
    per volume

Community Theatre Structure (written by W. Edwin Ver
    Becke)

Directory of Nonprofessional Community Theatres in the United States, 1952 (compiled by the Theatre and Adult Education Project of AETA), Price: 75¢ *

Foreign Information Centres

How to Build an Audience

How to Organize an Off-Broadway Theatre Group (edited by Ira J. Bilowit), Price: 50¢ *

How to Prepare a Résumé

Incorporation of Little Theatre Groups (written by William A. Dicker)

Initial Factors in Theatre Planning (written by James H. Miller and Members of the Theatre Architecture Project of AETA)

International Theatre Institute

Literature of the American Theatre, 1945-1956 (compiled by Elizabeth P. Barrett)

Literature on How to Organize and Operate a Community Theatre

National Centres of the International Theatre Institute

Periodicals of the Theatre

Play Publishers and Distributors

Pre-Sales Plan for Selling Blocks of Theatre Tickets

Schools of the Theatre

Sources for Special Plays and Play Lists

Suggestions for Play Contest Rules

Suggested Reading on Acting (compiled by Marjorie L. Dycke)

Suggested Reading in Theatre Architecture (compiled by the Theatre Architecture Project of AETA)

Summary of Basic Insurances to Cover Production Operation by a Resident Theatre (written by Harry L. Simon)

Theatre and Youth International Bibliography, Volume I (published by the International Theatre Institute), Price: 50¢ *

Theatre and Youth International Bibliography, Volume II (published by the International Theatre Institute), Price: 50¢ *

Theatre for Your City, A (published by Actors' Equity Association)

Theatrical Directories Available for Distribution

An Alphabetical List of Periodicals Of and About Theatre

CRITICAL DIGEST
139 East 47 Street, New York 17, New York
Weekly. Subscription, $25.00 per year; $10.00 per year for libraries; no single copies sold; free sample upon request. Weekly digests of New York City theatre reviews. News, drama, book, record, ticket, out-of-town and summer theatre reports.

CUE: *The Magazine of New York Living*
6 East 39 Street, New York 16, New York
Weekly. Subscription, $5.50 per year; 25 cents single copy. Includes listings of the events of the week in the theatre, sports, radio, television, and films; also reviews of stage, screen, radio, and television.

DANCE MAGAZINE
231 West 58 Street, New York 19, New York
Monthly. Subscription, $5.00 per year; 50 cents single copy. News, reviews, features—of ballet, concert, theatre, ball-

---

* Prices quoted are for ANTA members only. Non-members are charged a modest fee.

room, television and film dance; includes a "Young Dancer" section.

DANCE NEWS
119 West 57 Street, New York 19, New York
Monthly, except July and August. Subscription, $3.00 per year; 25 cents single copy. A monthly newspaper devoted to dance; national and international news coverage; performance and book reviews, feature articles.

DANCE OBSERVER
55 West 11 Street, New York 11, New York
Monthly from September to May; bi-monthly from June to September. Subscription, $2.00 per year; 25 cents single copy. Reviews of New York dance programs, dance in Broadway productions, dance recitals in colleges and universities.

DRAMATICS: *An Educational Magazine for Directors, Teachers and Students of Dramatic Arts*
Dramatics, College Hill Station, Cincinnati 24, Ohio
Eight times a year, October through May. Subscription, $2.50 per year; Thespian Sponsors, free; Thespian Students, $1.50 per year; 50 cents single copy. The official publication of the National Thespian Society, dedicated to the advancement of dramatic arts in education and recreation. Includes stage, screen and TV reviews, "how-to-do-it" articles, and news notes of member Thespian Troupes.

EDUCATIONAL THEATRE JOURNAL
Published by American Educational Theatre Association. Executive Office: American Educational Theatre Association, Executive Secretary, University Theatre, University of Minnesota, Minneapolis 14, Minnesota.
Quarterly, March, May, October and December. Subscription, $4.50 per year; $1.50 single copy; (included in membership to AETA, $5.50 per year). Official publication of the American Educational Theatre Association. Includes stage reviews, book reviews, research and surveys in the

educational theatre field, news notes of college and university theatre activity.

EQUITY

226 West 47 Street, New York 36, New York

Monthly. Subscription, $1.00 per year to Equity Members; $2.00 per year to non-members; 25 cents single copy. The official publication of the professional actors' union, The Actors' Equity Association.

NEW YORK THEATRE CRITICS' REVIEW

Critics' Theatre Reviews, Incorporated, 235 East 22 Street, New York 10, New York.

Weekly. Subscription, $25.00 year. Each issue reprints complete reviews by the New York drama critics as they appeared in the following New York daily newspapers: Journal-American, Daily News, Post, Mirror, World Telegram and Sun, Herald Tribune, Times.

OPERA NEWS

Metropolitan Opera Guild, 654 Madison Avenue, New York 21, New York

Weekly during the Opera Season and fortnightly Spring and Fall. Subscription, $4.00 per year; 20 cents single copy. Although primarily devoted to the Metropolitan Opera in New York, this illustrated magazine covers opera news and criticism of productions and personalities in other cities and countries, on radio, television and the screen.

PLAYERS MAGAZINE

P. O. Box 339, Gainesville, Florida

Eight times a year, October through May. Subscription, $3.50 per year; 50 cents single copy. The publication of the National Collegiate Players. Includes book and play reviews; material on educational and community theatre; sections on make-up, scenery, costumes, puppets, etc.

PLAYS

Plays, Incorporated, 8 Arlington Street, Boston 16, Massachusetts

Eight times a year, October through May. Subscription,

$5.00 per year; 75 cents single copy. Each issue contains 10 to 12 new plays written for primary and intermediate grades, junior and senior high school. Subscribers are permitted to perform the plays royalty free. The drama magazine for young people.

QUARTERLY JOURNAL OF SPEECH
Executive Office: Speech Association of America, Waldo W. Braden, Executive Secretary, Louisiana State University, Baton Rouge 3, Louisiana
Quarterly, February, April, October, December. Subscription, $4.50 per year; special subscriptions for undergraduates, $3.50 per year; $1.25 single copy. Abstracts, bibliographies, book reviews, research, critical studies on all phases of speech, speech training, speech and the theatre.

SHAKESPEARE NEWSLETTER
% Louis Marder, Kent State University, Kent, Ohio.
Six times a year, February, April, May, September, November, December. Subscription, $1.00 per year. Reports on Shakespearean productions in professional, college and community theatres, on radio and television. Bibliographies and reviews of books and periodical articles dealing with Shakespeare; articles and news notes.

SHAKESPEARE QUARTERLY
Publisher: Shakespeare Association of America, Incorporated, 322 East 57 Street, New York, New York.
Quarterly. Subscriptions, $5.00 per year; $1.50 single copy. Research, criticism, book and performance reviews of interest to the Shakespeare student and scholar. The winter issue includes an international round-up of Shakespeare productions.

THEATRE ARTS
130 West 56 Street, New York 19, New York
Monthly. Subscription, $5.00 per year; $9.00 for two years; 50 cents single copy. National coverage of professional theatre; reviews of Broadway productions, theatre books and records; includes feature articles and criticism, college

and community theatre section. Each issue contains the complete text of a recent Broadway play.

VARIETY
154 West 46 Street, New York 36, New York
Weekly. Subscription, $10.00 per year; 25 cents single copy. *Variety* includes stage, screen, radio, TV, night club, vaudeville, record, orchestra reviews and news coverage of professional theatre, national and international (films, radio, video, music, stage).

WORLD PREMIERES
International Theatre Institute, 19 Avenue Kleber, Paris, France. Andre Josset, Secretary-General.
Subscription Office, U.S.; ANTA, 1545 Broadway, New York 36, New York
Monthly bulletin of the International Theatre Institute, ten times a year, excluding August and September. Subscription, available through ANTA membership, $6.00 per year. Credit listings, plot precis and critical summaries of the new productions (world premieres) opening in the member countries of the International Theatre Institute.

WORLD THEATRE
Published under the auspices of UNESCO and the International Theatre Institute, 19 Avenue Kleber, Paris, France
Quarterly. Subscription, $3.50 per year; $1.00 single copy. Illustrated review containing valuable information and comment of theatre the world over; printed in French and English.

For Further Reading

A selected list of books about theatre—some for information and some for entertainment

Theatre History

Blum, Daniel, *A Pictorial History of the American Theatre,* Rev. Ed. 4th. New York: Greenberg, 1956.

Brown, John Mason, *The Modern Theatre in Revolt.* New York: W. W. Norton & Company, Inc., 1929.

Clark, Barrett H. and George Freedley, *A History of Modern Drama.* New York: Appleton-Century-Crofts, Inc., 1947.

Clurman, Harold, *The Fervent Years.* New York: Alfred A. Knopf, Inc., 1950.

Freedley, George and John A. Reeves, *A History of the Theatre,* Rev. Ed. New York: Crown Publishers, Inc., 1955.

Hughes, Glenn, *A History of the American Theatre,* 1700-1950. New York: Samuel French, Inc., 1951.

The Technical Side—More or Less

Archer, William and Harley Granville-Barker, *Schemes and Estimates for A National Theatre.* New York: Duffield and Company, 1908.

Calvert, Louis, *Problems of the Actor.* New York: Henry Holt and Co., Inc., 1918.

Cheney, Sheldon, *The Theatre,* Rev. Ed. New York: Longmans, Green & Co., Inc., 1958.

———, *The Art Theatre,* Rev. & Enlarged Ed. New York: Alfred A. Knopf, Inc., 1925.

Chekhov, Mikhail, *To the Actor.* New York: Harper & Brothers, 1953.

Chorpenning, Charlotte, *Twenty-One Years with Children's Theatre*. Anchorage, Kentucky: Children's Theatre Press, 1954.

Egri, Lajos, *The Art of Dramatic Writing*, Rev. Ed. New York: Simon and Schuster, Inc., 1946.

Gibson, William, *The Seesaw Log*. New York: Alfred A. Knopf, Inc., 1959.

Goodman, Edward, *Make Believe: The Art of Acting*. New York: Charles Scribner's Sons, 1956.

Hopkins, Arthur, *Reference Point*. New York: Samuel French, Inc., 1948.

Houghton, Norris, *Moscow Rehearsals*. New York: Harcourt, Brace & Co., 1936.

Jones, Margo, *Theatre in the Round*. New York: Rinehart & Company, Inc., 1951.

Jones, Robert Edmond, *The Dramatic Imagination*. New York: Theatre Arts Books, 1956.

Macgowan, Kenneth and William Melnitz, *The Living Stage: A History of the World Theatre*. New York: Prentice-Hall, Inc., 1955.

Sayler, Oliver, *Inside the Moscow Art Theatre*. New York: Brentano's, 1925.

Simonson, Lee, *The Stage Is Set*. New York: Harcourt, Brace & Co., 1932.

———, *Part of a Lifetime*. New York: Duell, Sloan & Pearce, Inc., 1943.

Stanislavsky, Constantin, *Building a Character*. New York: Theatre Arts Books, 1949.

———, *My Life in Art*. Boston: Little, Brown & Co., 1924.

———, *An Actor Prepares*. New York: Theatre Arts Books, 1955.

Talma, Francois Joseph, *Reflexions on the Actor's Art*. New York: Dramatic Museum of Columbia University, 1915.

Van Druten, John, *Playwright at Work*. New York: Harper & Brothers, 1952.

Light and Sidelights on Various Aspects of Theatre

Bentley, Eric, *In Search of Theater*. New York: Vintage Books, Inc., 1954.

Bernhardt, Sarah, *The Art of the Theatre*. London: Geoffrey Bles Ltd., 1924.

Clark, Barrett H., *Eugene O'Neill: The Man and His Plays*, Rev. Version. New York: Dover Publications, Inc., 1947.

Granville-Barker, Harley, *Prefaces to Shakespeare*. Princeton: Princeton University Press, 1946.

James, Henry, *The Scenic Art*. New Brunswick: Rutgers University Press, 1948.

———, *The Tragic Muse*. Boston & New York: Houghton Mifflin Co., 1890.

Oppenheimer, George, *The Passionate Playgoer: A Personal Scrapbook*. New York: The Viking Press, Inc., 1958.

Seldes, Gilbert, *The Seven Lively Arts*, Enlarged Ed. New York: Sagamore Press, Inc., 1957.

Shaw, George Bernard, *Dramatic Opinions and Essays*. New York: Brentano's, 1906.

Woollcott, Alexander, *Mrs. Fiske*. New York: The Century Co., 1917.

———, *Enchanted Aisles*. New York & London: G. P. Putnam's Sons, 1924.

Young, Stark, *The Flower in Drama and Glamour*. New York: Charles Scribner's Sons, 1955.

On Community Theatre

Houghton, Norris, *Advance from Broadway—19,000 Miles of American Theatre*. New York: Harcourt, Brace & Co., 1941.

McCleery, Albert and Carl Glick, *Curtains Going Up*. New York & Chicago: Pitman Publishing Corp., 1939.

Selden, Samuel, *Organizing a Community Theatre*. Cleveland: National Theatre Conference, 1945.

Young, John Wray, *The Community Theatre*. New York: Harper & Brothers, 1957.

Biographies and Autobiographies

Armstrong, Margaret, *Fanny Kemble, A Passionate Victorian*. New York: The Macmillan Co., 1938.

Bailey, Mabel Driscoll, *Maxwell Anderson, The Playwright as Prophet*. New York: Abelard-Schuman, Limited, 1957.

Belmont, Eleanor Robson, *The Fabric of Memory*. New York: Farrar, Straus and Cudahy, Inc., 1957.

Boulton, Agnes, *Part of a Long Story*. Garden City: Doubleday & Company, Inc., 1958.

Courtney, Marguerite, *Laurette*. New York: Rinehart & Company, Inc., 1955.

DeMille, Agnes, *Dance to the Piper*. Boston: Little, Brown & Co., 1952.

Duncan, Isadora, *My Life*. New York: Liveright Publishing Corp., 1933.

Freedley, George, *The Lunts*. London: Rockliff Publishing Corp., 1957.

Le Gallienne, Eva, *At 33*. New York & Toronto: Longmans, Green & Co., Inc., 1934.

———, *With a Quiet Heart*. New York: The Viking Press, Inc., 1953.

161

O'Casey, Sean, *Mirror in My House*. New York: The Macmillan Co., 1956.

Robbins, Phyllis, *Maude Adams*. New York: G. P. Putnam's Sons, 1956.

Row, Arthur William, *Sarah the Divine*. New York: Comet Press Books, 1957.

Tynan, Kenneth, *Alec Guinness*. London: Rockliff Publishing Corp., 1954.

Verneuil, Louis, *The Fabulous Life of Sarah Bernhardt*. New York and London: Harper & Brothers, 1942.

Waters, Ethel, with Charles Samuels, *His Eye Is on the Sparrow*. Garden City: Doubleday & Company, Inc., 1951.

Some Highly Personal Preferences— A Miscellaneous Collection

Brahms, Caryl and S. J. Simon, *Six Curtains for Stroganova*. London: Michael Joseph, Ltd., 1945.

Chute, Marchette, *Shakespeare of London*. New York: E. P. Dutton & Co., Inc., 1949.

———, *The Wonderful Winter*. New York: E. P. Dutton & Co., 1954.

Dane, Clemence, *Broome Stages*. London: William Heinemann, Ltd., 1931.

D'Annunzio, Gabriele, *The Flame of Life*. New York: Boni & Liveright, 1919.

Hamilton, Edith, *The Great Age of Greek Literature*. New York: W. W. Norton & Company, Inc., 1942.

Karsavina, Tamara, *Theatre Street: The Reminiscences of Tamara Karsavina*. New York: E. P. Dutton & Co.. Inc., 1931.

Index

165

167